THE CLUB OF NINE

Lafite

THE CLUB OF NINE

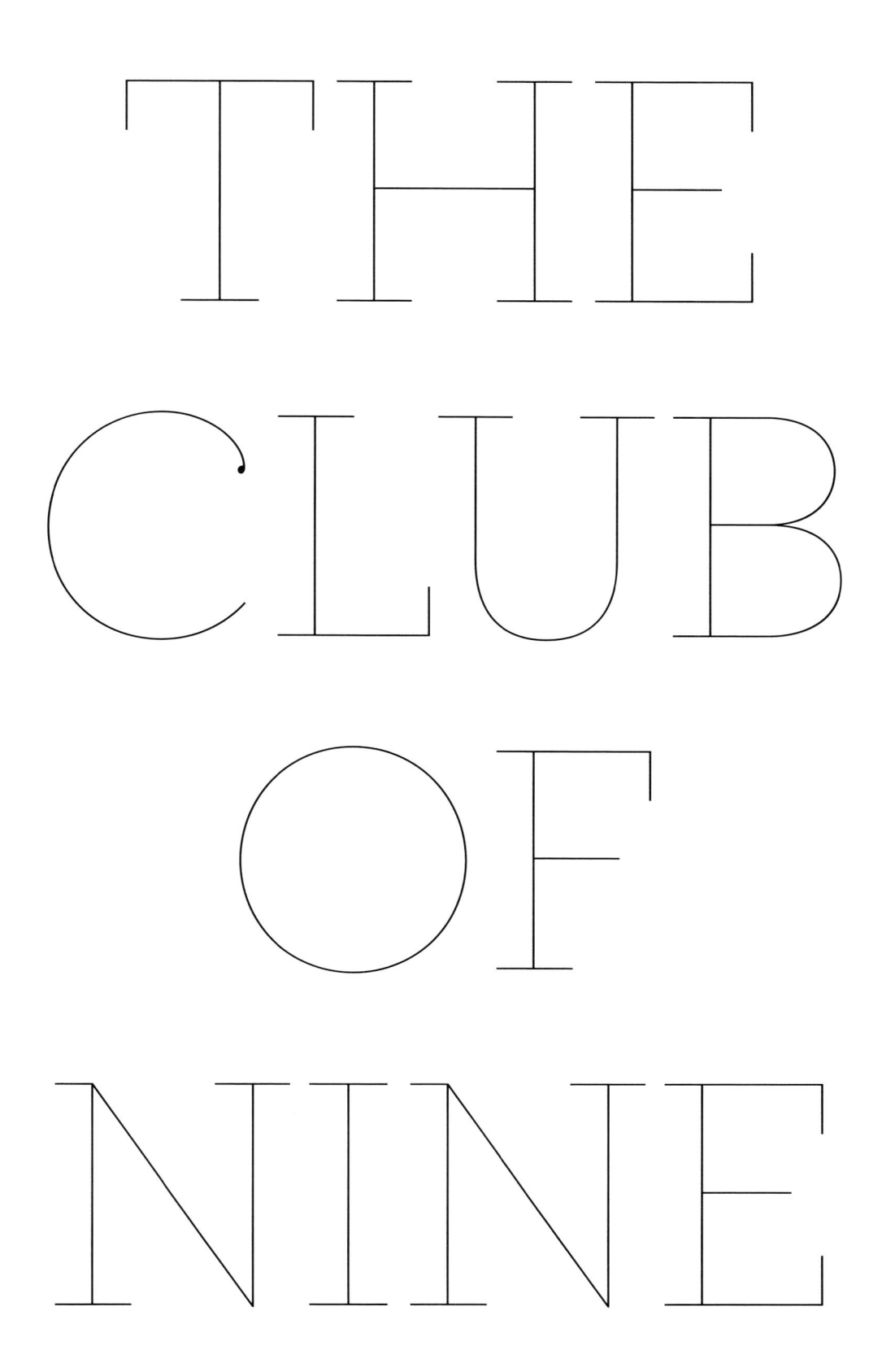

Photography by Andy Katz
Words by Jane Anson

THE CLUB OF NINE

INSIDE THE GREATEST
WINES OF BORDEAUX

LAFITE ROTHSCHILD
LATOUR
MARGAUX
MOUTON ROTHSCHILD
HAUT-BRION
YQUEM
PETRUS
CHEVAL BLANC
AUSONE

INTRODUCTION

There are no rules for entry to this club. Not ones, at least, that you can look up. There's no membership card, no annual fee. No amount of picking apart the list of members will tell you exactly how they got in. And yet, this is without question the most exclusive set of names in wine. Perhaps in any industry. Not just at the top of their game but the definition of it.

Nine châteaux, with enough music in their syllables to fire up an orchestra. Six on the Left Bank of Bordeaux, three on the Right Bank. If we list them from north to south we get Lafite Rothschild, Mouton Rothschild, Latour, Margaux, Haut-Brion and Yquem on the Left; Petrus, Cheval Blanc and Ausone on the Right.

In total, they represent 1,437 acres of vines, with the smallest standing at just 17 acres and the largest at 279. Every inch is the easy equivalent of New York's Upper East Side, Russia's Yubileyny diamond mine, Mark Rothko's multiform canvases.

Together they are known as the First Growths of Bordeaux – the greatest wines of a region that gave birth to the idea of a global fine wine market. And yet even this is a red herring. Five were anointed First Growths in 1855, two in 1955, one in 1973. The last has no official ranking and yet shares every bit of the magnetism.

Better, then, to think of them as the Club of Nine, drawn together by something bigger and more immutable than a date or a title. Each one has achieved what they have through adherence to a single big idea – proof that there are no limits to what any of us can achieve if we keep pushing.

Not one of these estates woke up one day to be declared great. They are the sum of successive owners believing in the potential of individual pieces of land. Owners who have proved themselves willing to commit resources, time, skills and energy to surviving whatever has been thrown at them. They are the history of bankruptcies, wars, revolutions and stubborn single-mindedness.

It's no exaggeration to say that you can trace the history of Bordeaux through the timeline of these properties. Let's go further, and say you can read the history of modern wine in their libraries, cellars and vineyards. Not just in theory, but in fact – from the simple idea of associating a specific place and property name with an individual wine, to the benefits of barrel ageing and estate bottling.

Let's pick out a few highlights from the saga of Bordeaux and see how they fit in.

The Romans, no surprises here, were the first to regularly plant vines in the region more than 2,000 years ago. And there is plenty of evidence to suggest that the first vines were planted around the city walls of Bordeaux – or Burdigala as it was known then – near spots today occupied by Château Haut-Brion. By the second century of their reign, vines were planted on the limestone plateau of Saint Emilion where Château Ausone stands today. The significance of the Roman era is referenced in the name of this ancient Saint Emilion domain, which takes its inspiration from Emperor Ausonius, a statesman and poet who owned over 200 acres of vines in Bordeaux. And just down the road in Pomerol, a separate site was owned by a Roman named Petrus.

A millennia later, and it was the marriage of Eleanor of Aquitaine to King Henry II that made Bordeaux a duchy of the English crown and kick-started the region's rise to fine wine dominance. Here, too, you will find the Club of Nine. Legend has it that Eleanor stayed in the tower of Château Lafite (or the Seigneurie de La Hite as it was then) in 1150, just before divorcing her first husband and moving on to Henry.

This marriage led directly to the establishment of Bordeaux as an international wine centre, something that all nine of these properties have more than played their part in sustaining. For at least 400 years, ever since Haut-Brion set up the Pontack's Head tavern in Restoration London, the First Growths have been set in front of the most discerning palates of the day, from Charles II and Daniel Defoe in the 17th century to Thomas Jefferson in the 18th century and Russian tsars in the 19th. There's a thesis waiting to be written that extrapolates the dominant social group of the ages by tracing the most significant export destinations of the Club of Nine.

Away from the drinkers and on to the side of the owners, we have largely French families, although almost invariably with international influences. There's the Rothschild cousins at Lafite and Mouton; a Prince of Luxembourg at Haut-Brion; the Greek-French Mentzelopoulos family at Margaux; the almighty Moueix family at Petrus; the Vauthiers at Ausone. The last time any of the estates changed hands was back in the 1990s, when two luxury goods magnates bought into the club. François Pinault and Bernard Arnault (both French, although Arnault bought with his Belgian friend and fellow billionaire Albert Frère)

respectively secured Château Latour and both Châteaux d'Yquem and Cheval Blanc. Prices paid for club membership vary widely of course, as Mouton was secured by the Rothschilds in 1853 while Yquem was snapped up as recently as 1999, but no one doubts that today this is a billion euro club, should any come up for sale again.

Yet beyond all of this, beyond the history, the owners, the money and the adulation, there is the wine.

It is here that all of the noise fades away. Each estate becomes an ongoing conversation between pieces of land and the people who inhabit them; land that has been shaped by the movements of the earth's crust and the changing climate over many millions of years, and the men and women who have slowly teased them into brilliance. Each has its own story, with some having to fight harder, or longer, to reach their potential.

Their very differences paint a picture of the complexity of the world's largest fine wine region. Located on different sides of Bordeaux's Garonne and Dordogne rivers, on soils that shift from gravel to clay to limestone to silex and through many fractions in-between, eight of the nine are famed for their red wines, crafted with a majority of merlot, cabernet sauvignon or cabernet franc. This befits a region that stands at nearly 90% red grapes. And yet among the nine is Château d'Yquem – producer of the most lyrical, luscious sweet white wine in the world, created by the magic of a rot that doesn't know it's supposed to be the enemy of quality winemaking. There are dry white wines among them also: Margaux, Mouton, Yquem and Haut-Brion sculpt sauvignon blanc and sémillon grapes into the finest examples of these grapes that you will find anywhere.

There is no recipe to how their wine is made, and no single link to be drawn between their soil structure and what is revealed in the final glass. If you follow the vine plants as they head underground, Lafite and Mouton have roots that go down six to eight metres through nearly pure gravel, while Latour and Petrus find their roots almost entirely blocked at two metres because the clay that underpins them is powerfully tight. Meanwhile, Yquem has sand and loam in key parts of its soil – something that typically is seen to give light, fragrant wines, yet anyone who has tasted a glass of this sublimely complex elixir would laugh at the thought.

The closest that we can come to an explanation of what makes their soils so propitious for greatness is that all are able to regulate the delivery of water to the vines, giving just enough but not too much. All truly exceptional wines the world over need to come from grapes that encounter a certain amount of struggling and resistance out in the vineyard. Although these nine estates have very different soil types, they all deliver the right amount of tough love.

What is also certain is that each wine can take your breath away in a single instant, and yet keep its counsel for years. They reward patience. Each has its distinctive signature, from the heady perfume of Margaux to the flamboyance of Mouton to the near-unbelievable ageing ability of Yquem. And each honours its history while still striving to push forward, millimetre by millimetre, to exceed the promise of its name.

This is why the Club of Nine is not only an idea but also a physical entity – a research and development programme initiated by these estates that began in a smaller form in the 1920s, disbanded in the 1950s, then took its current shape in the 1980s. The Club of Nine is not so much a cooperation between châteaux owners as between directors and technical staff, working alongside Bordeaux's Institute of Oenology to co-fund research for university doctorates and to explore key issues that each of them faces, from rootstock choices to oak selection for barrels to finding effective vineyard treatments within the confines of organic and biodynamic farming.

We could spend a highly pleasurable lifetime trying to understand why these nine properties stand out from the 8,000 or so châteaux that crowd this corner of south west France. The truth is there is no simple answer. Yet each member of this club stands as a symbol of the mastery of man over his environment, and of the transformation of wine from a drink of sustenance to something exceptional, inexpressible, magic. They give each of us the chance to brush against the infinite.

26 Margaux

Ausone

Latour

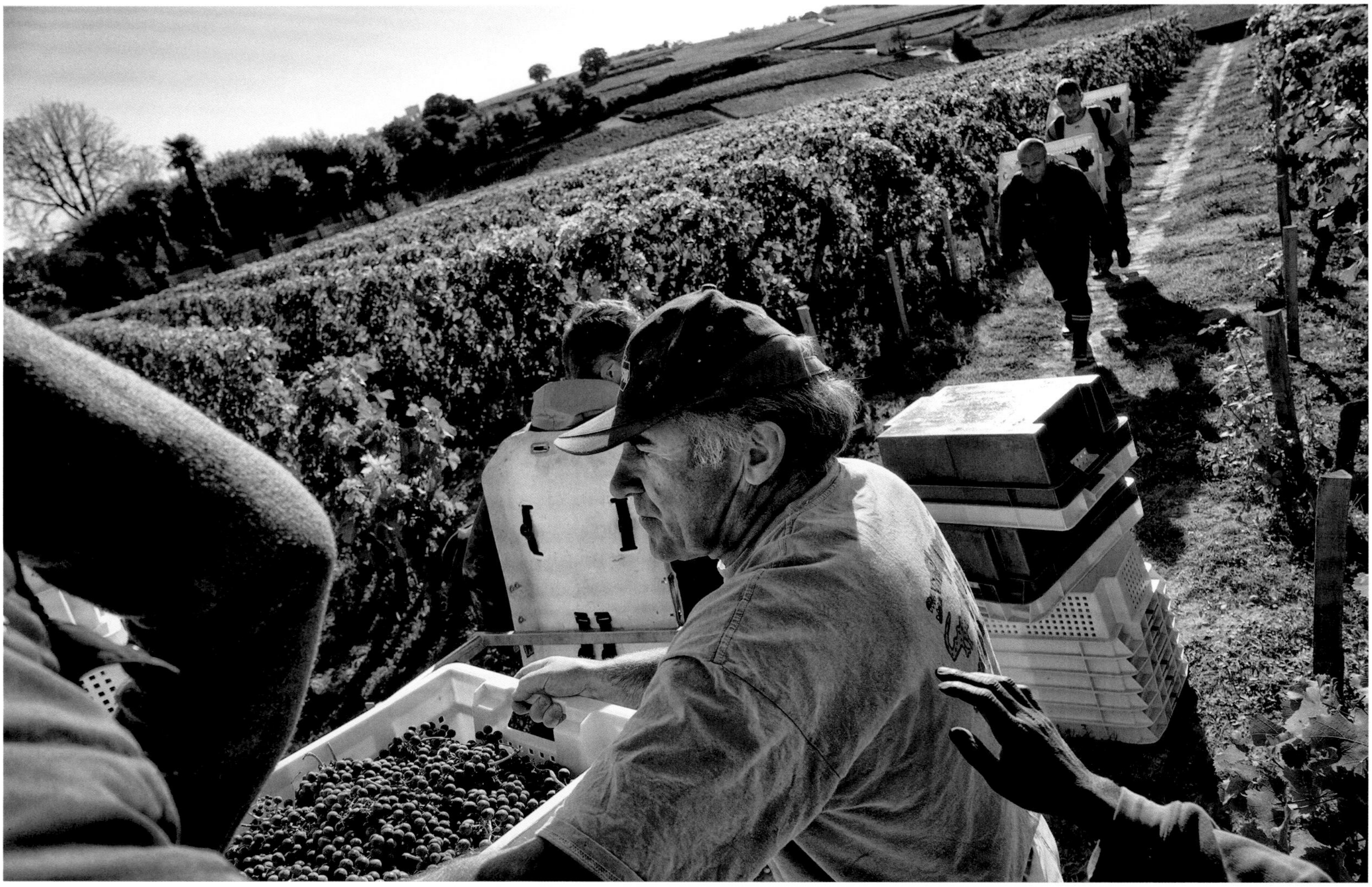

Lafite

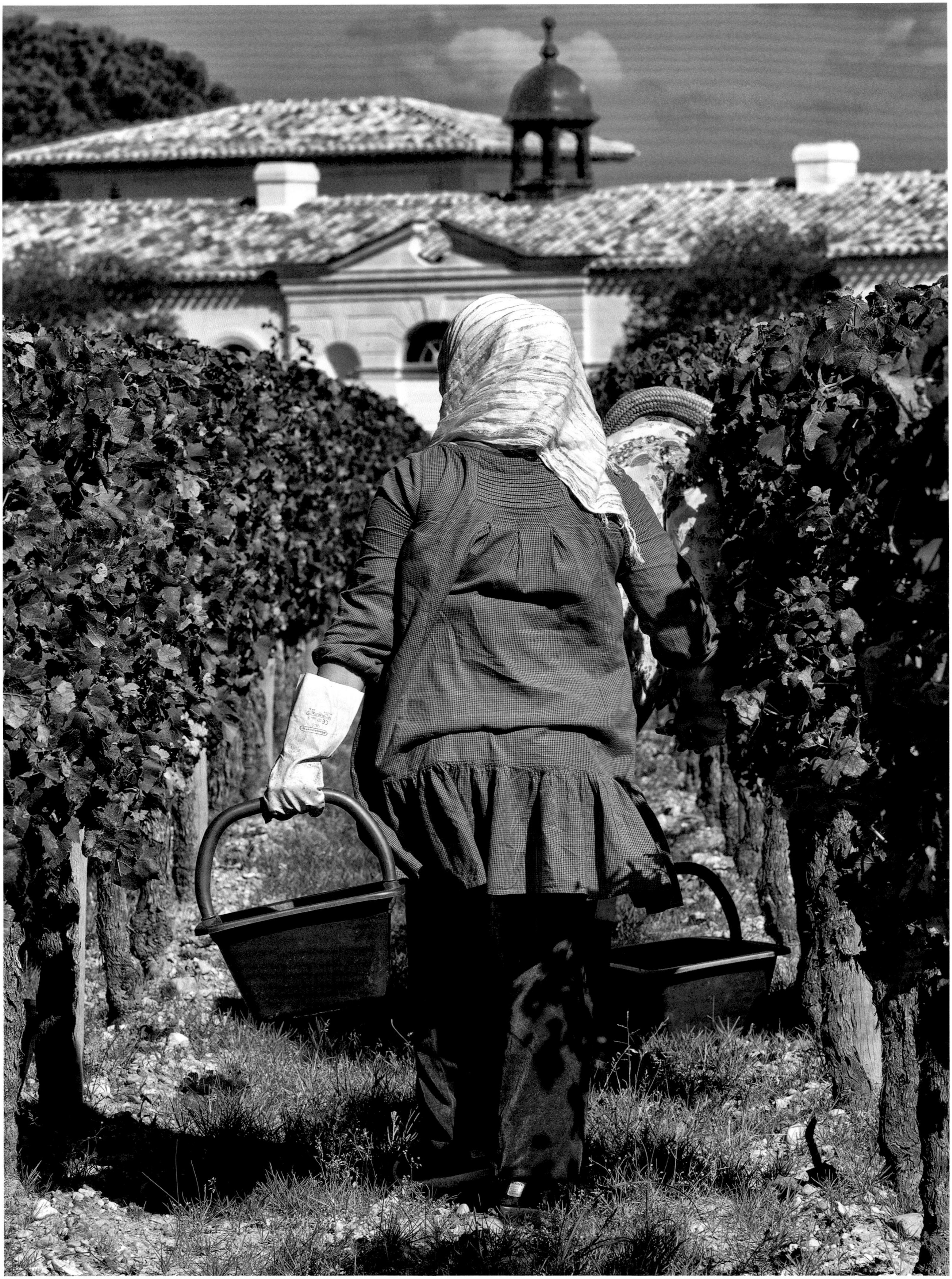

Petrus

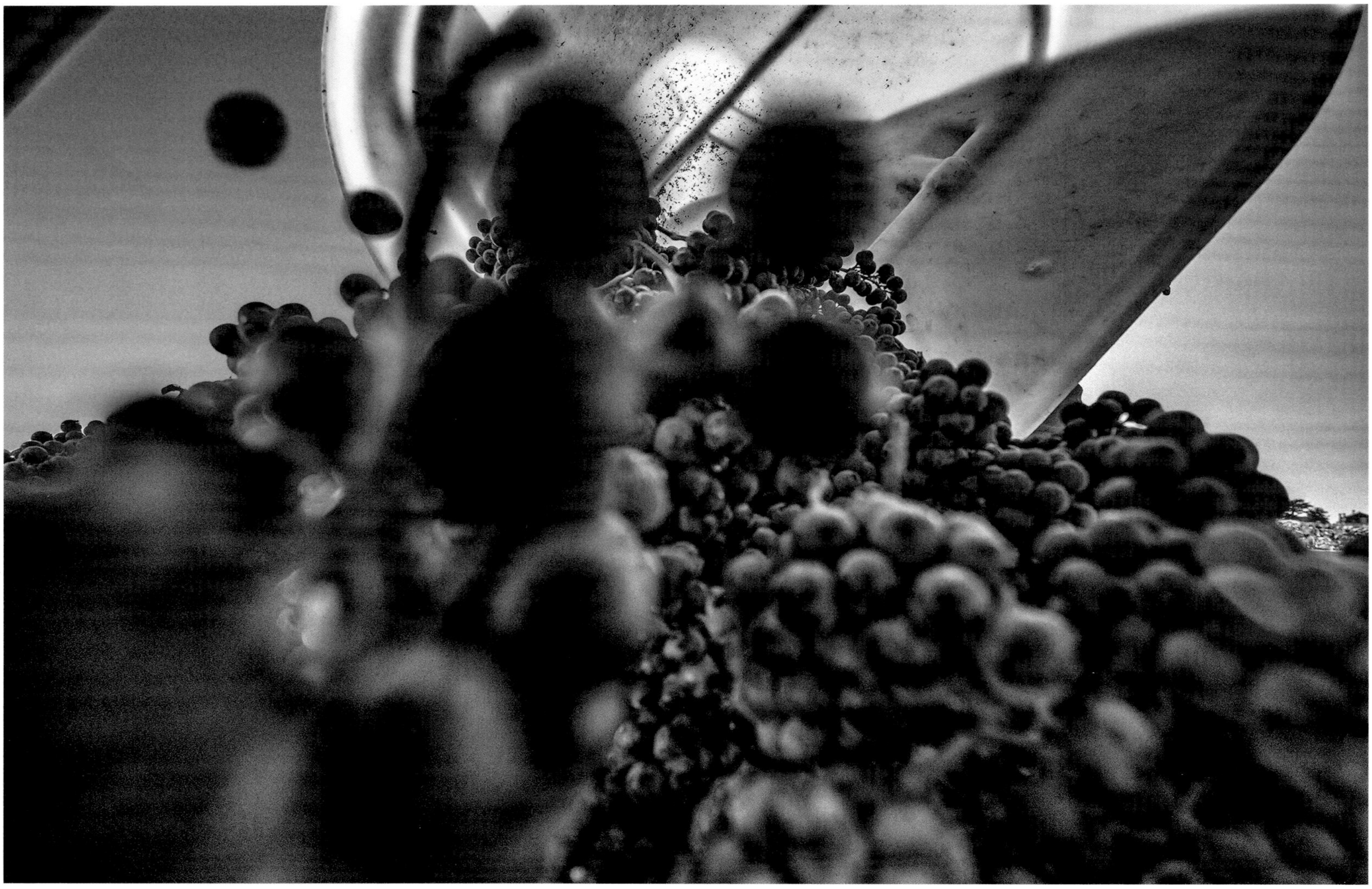

Petrus

Haut-Brion

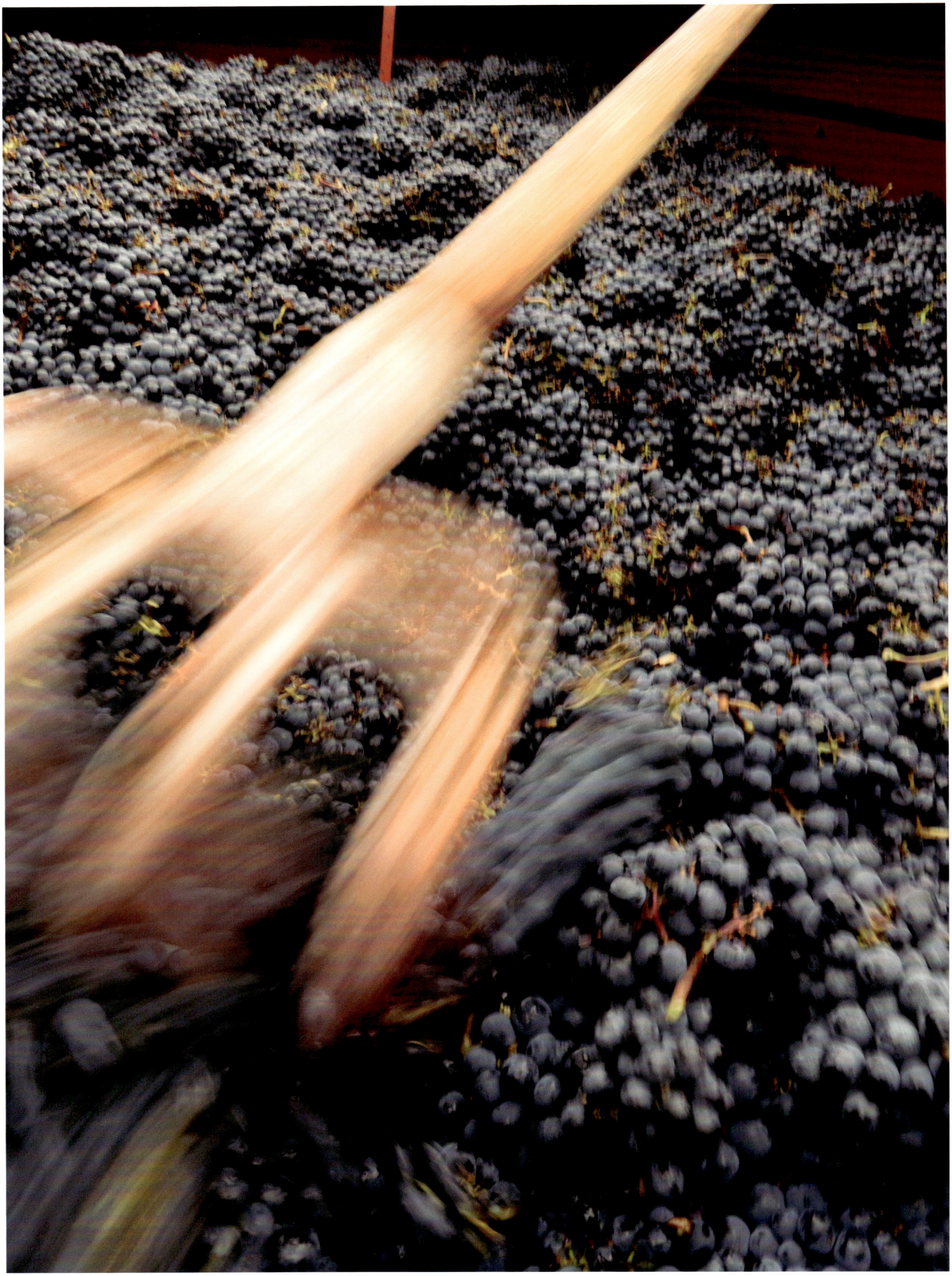

Cabernet

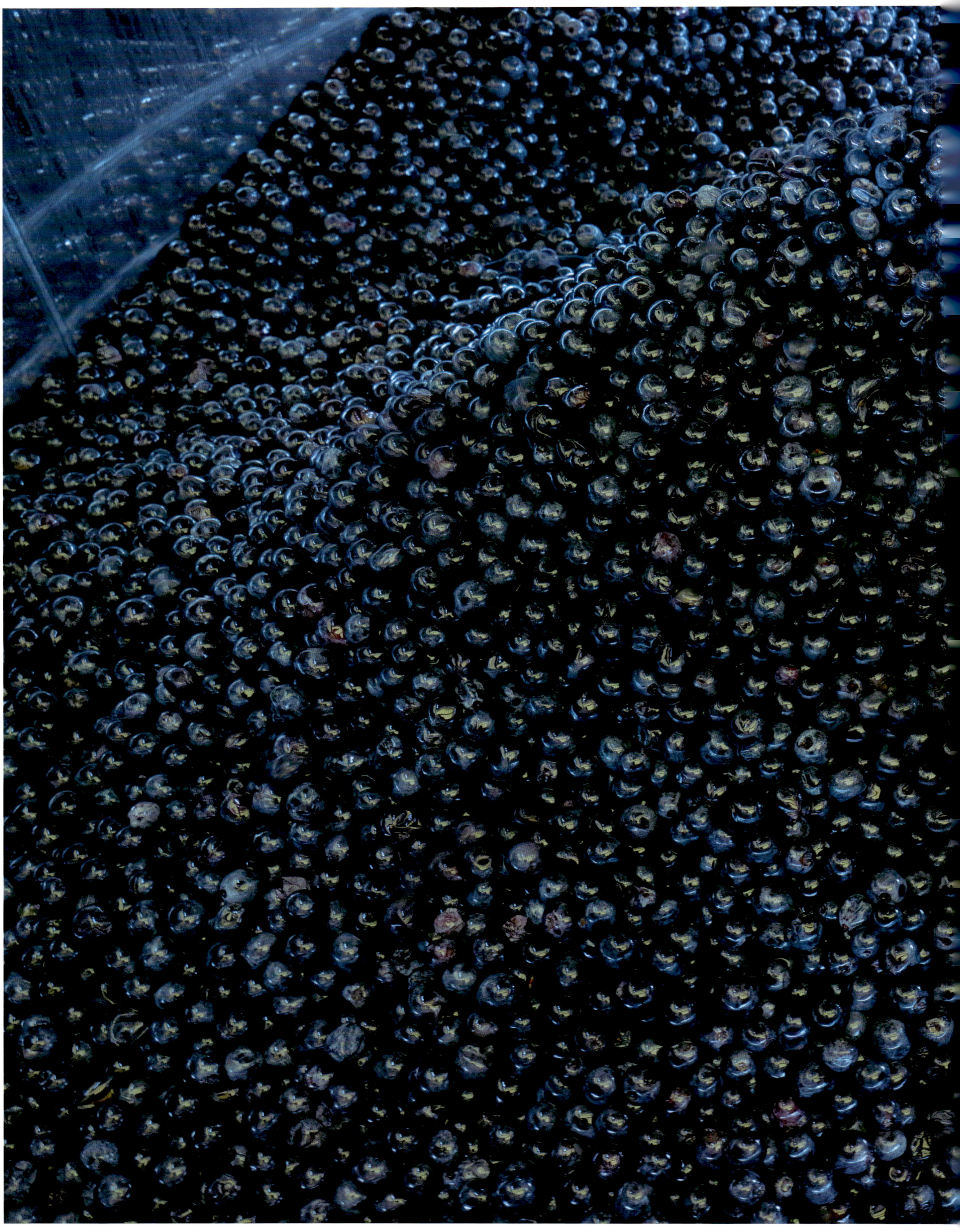

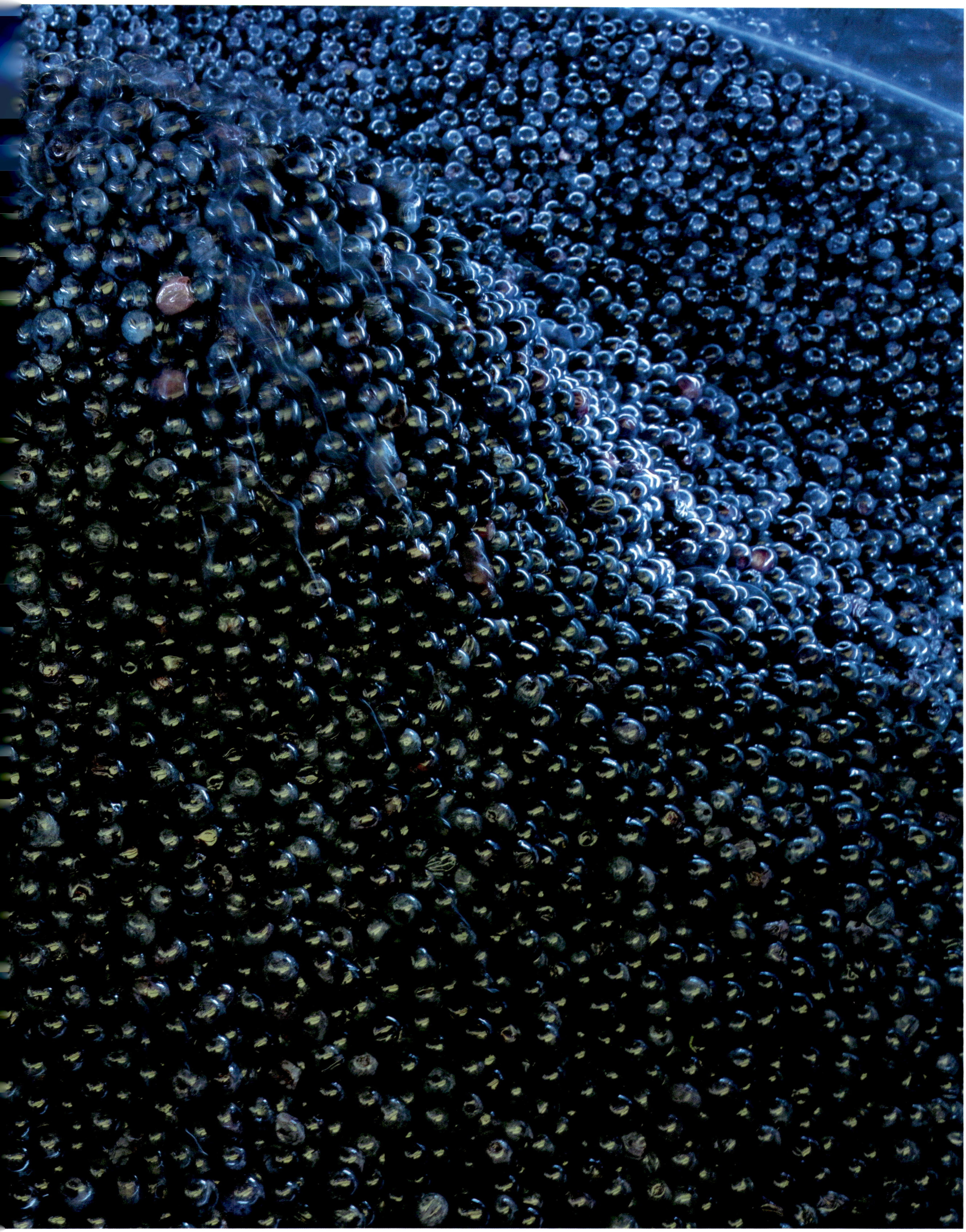

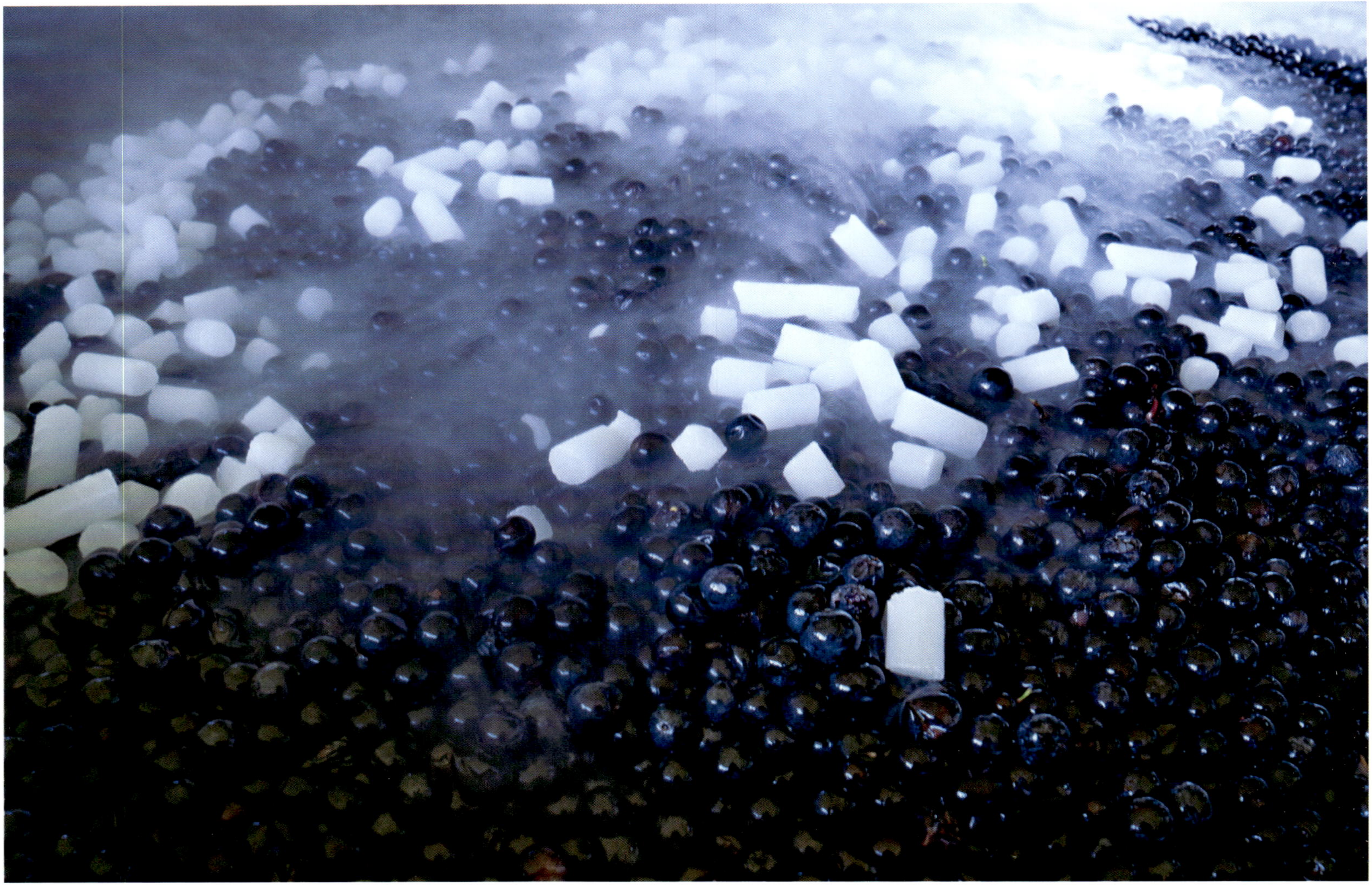

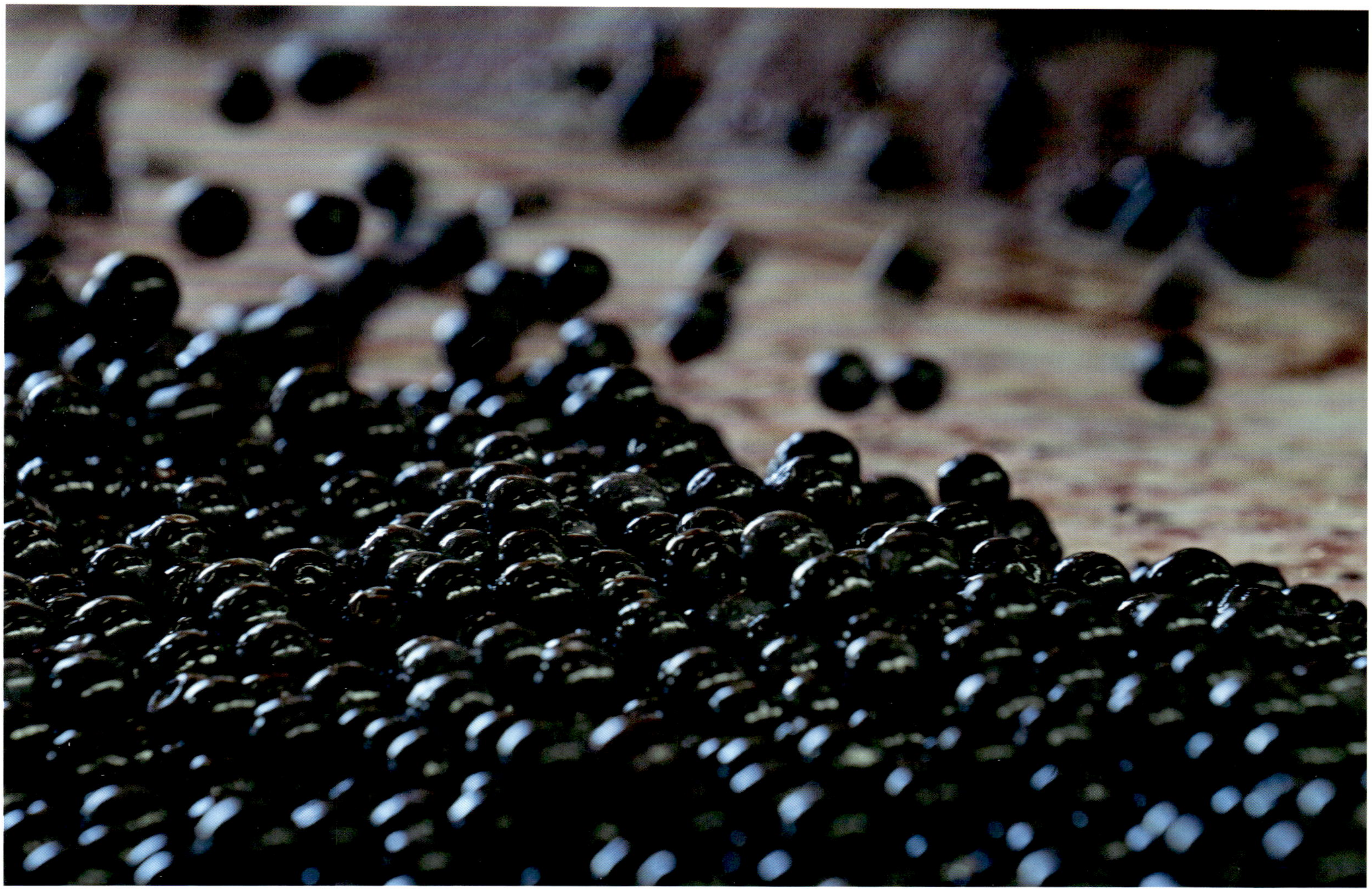

Cabernet Sauvignon

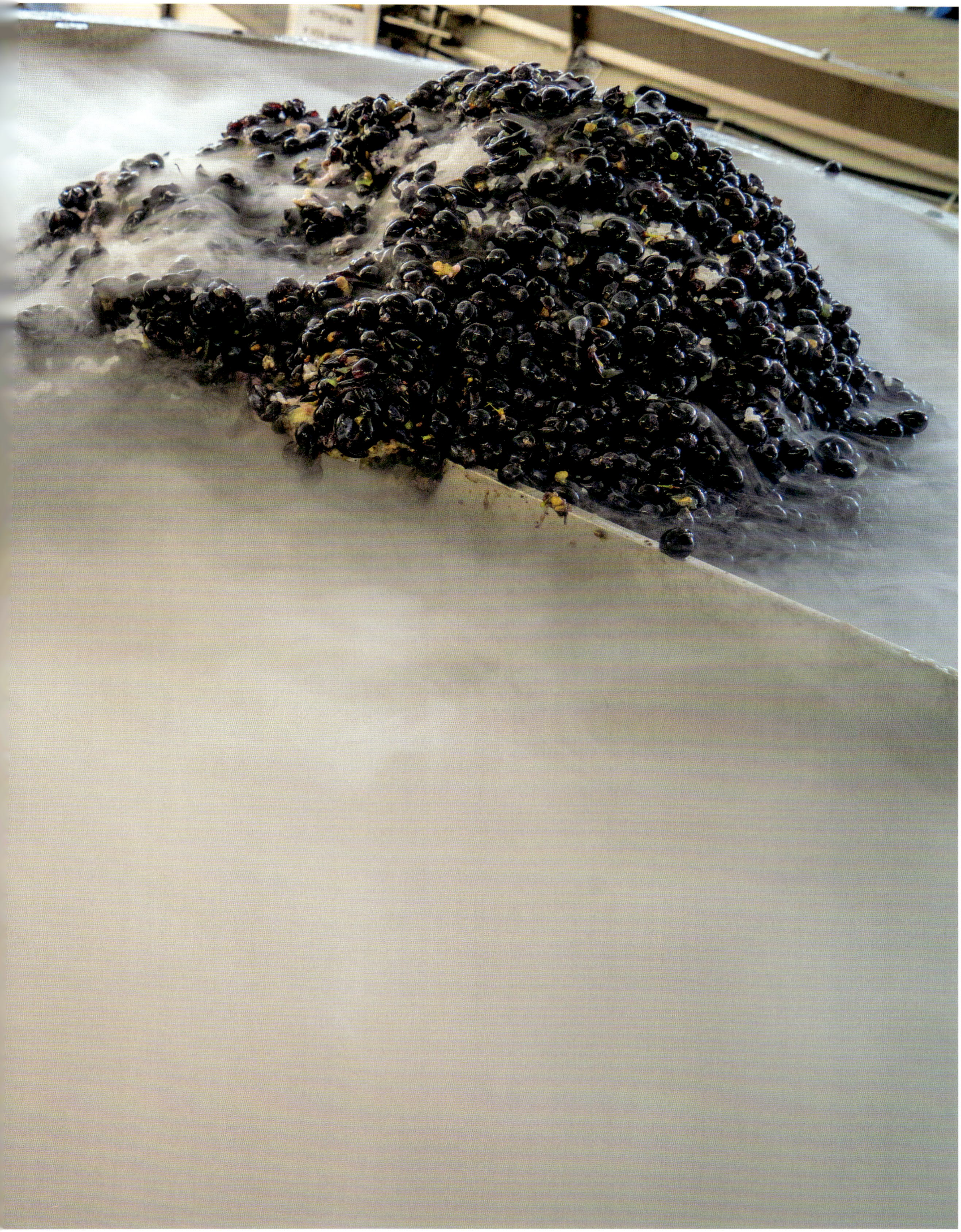

Merlot

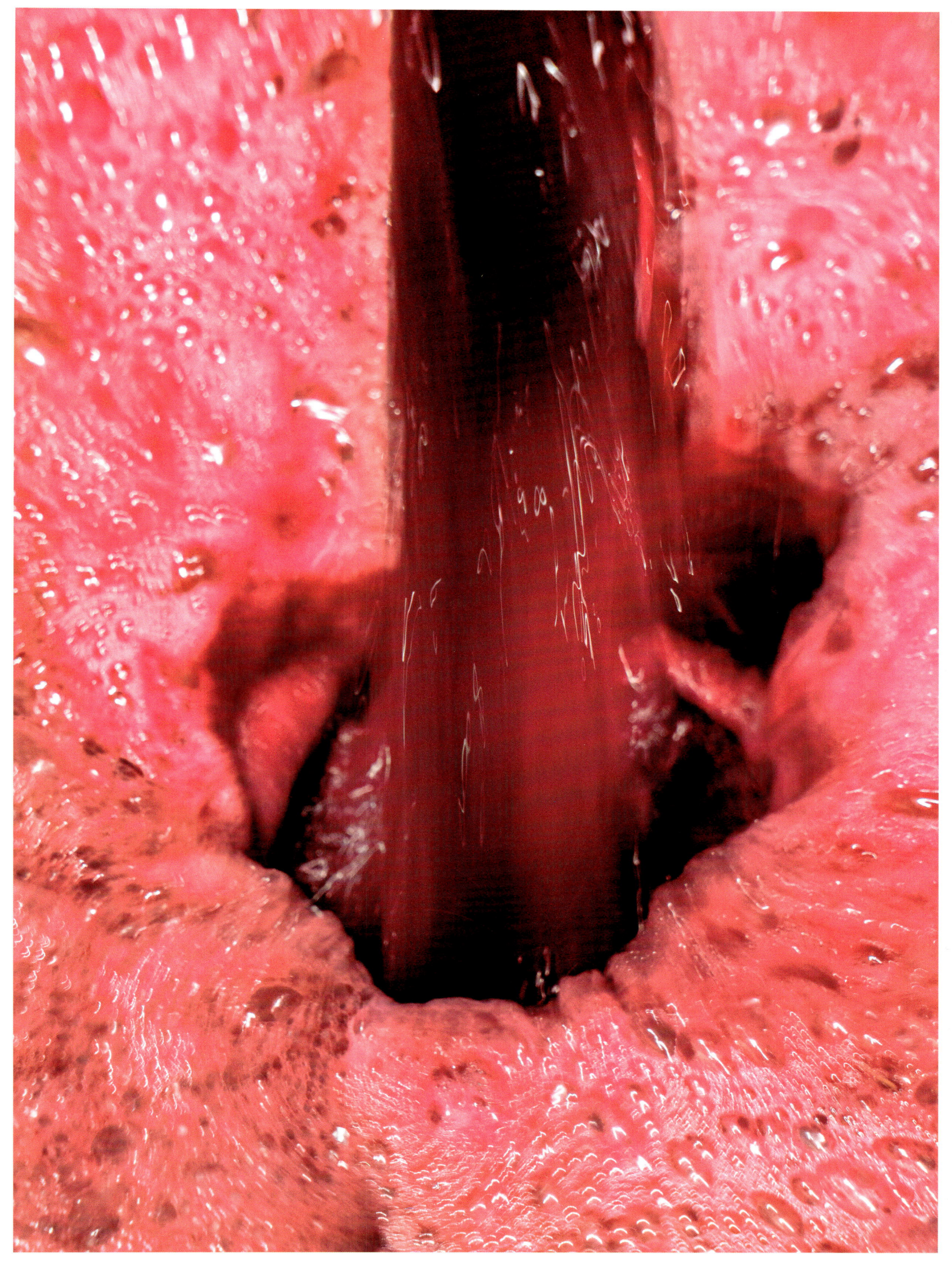

Cheval Blanc

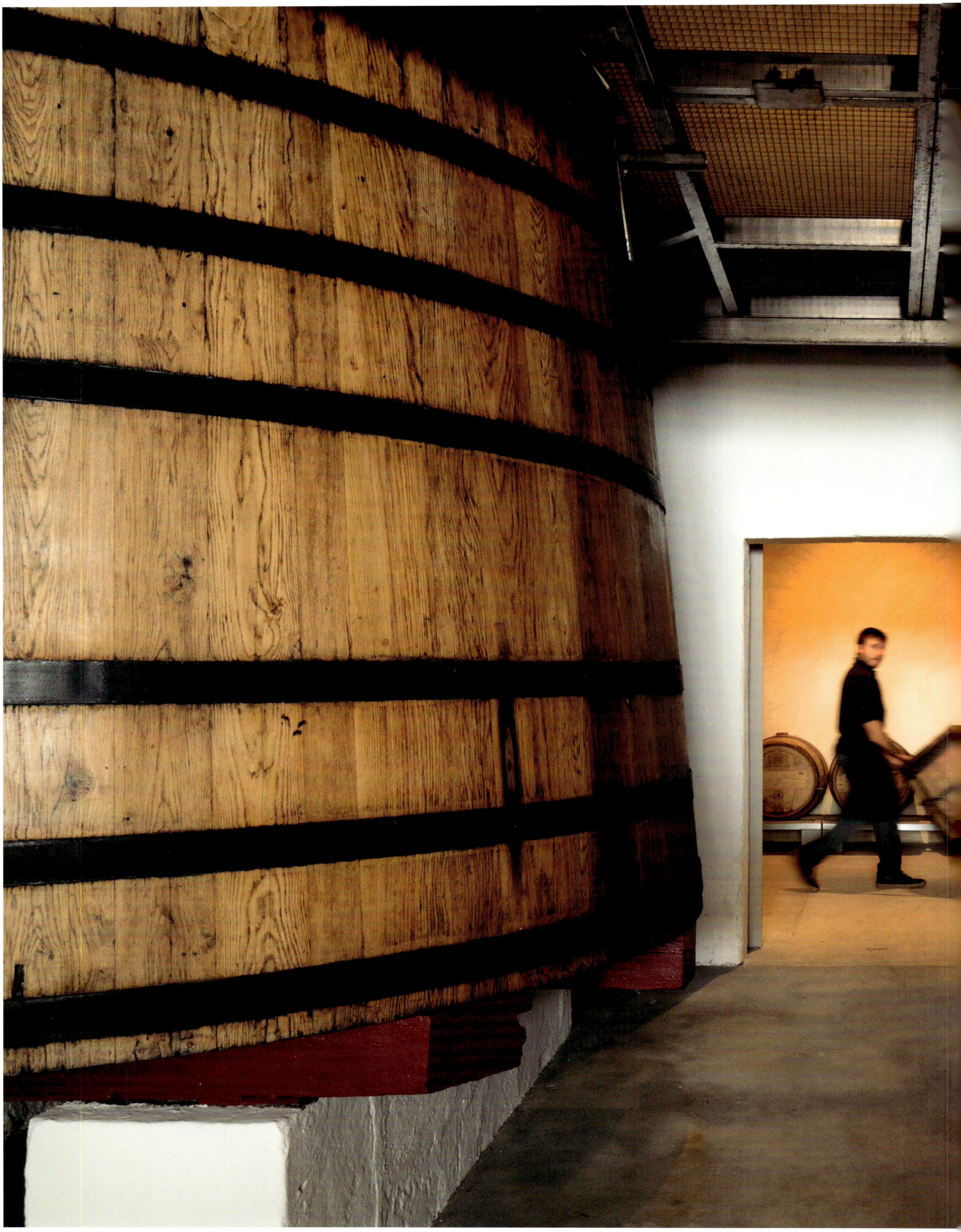

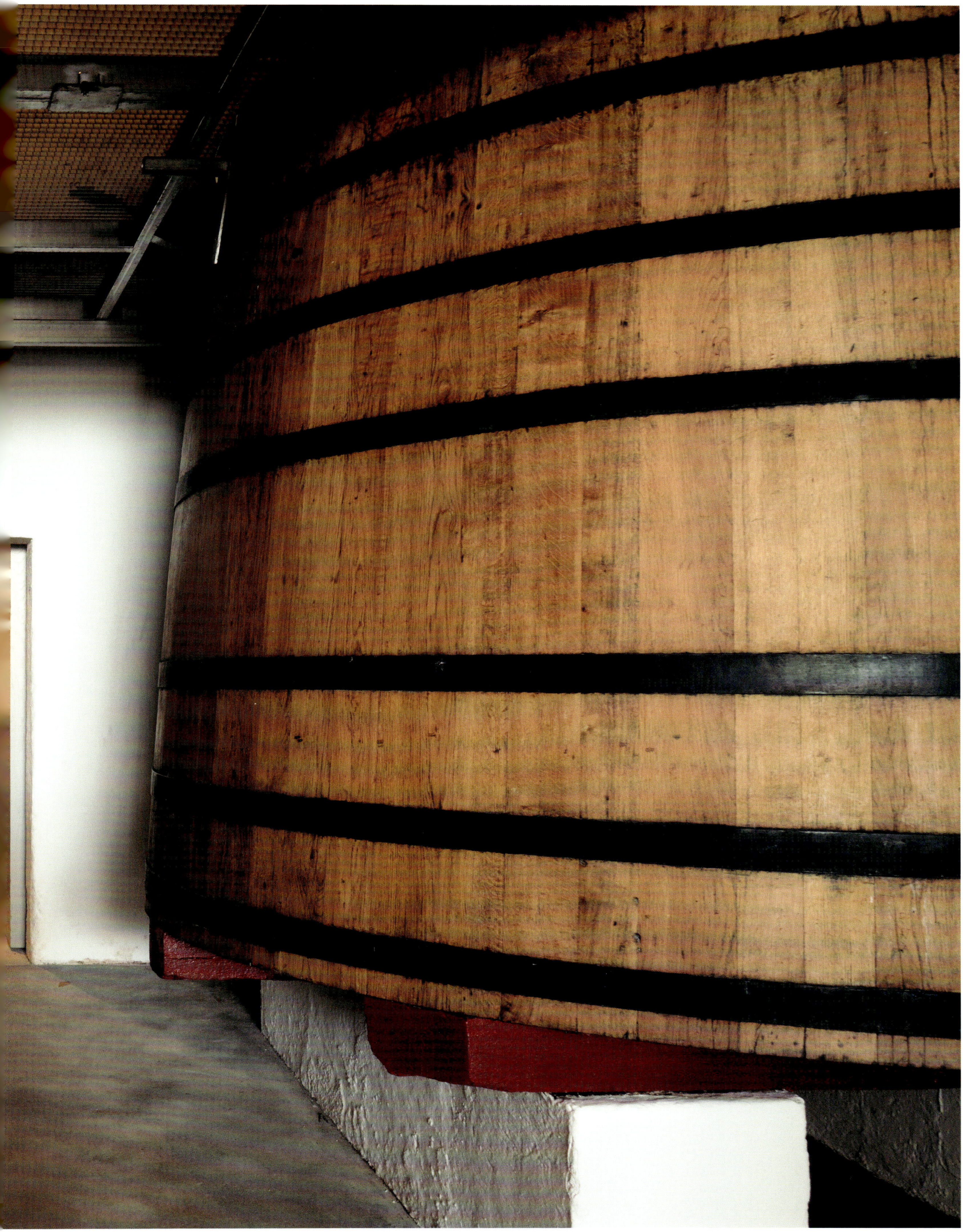

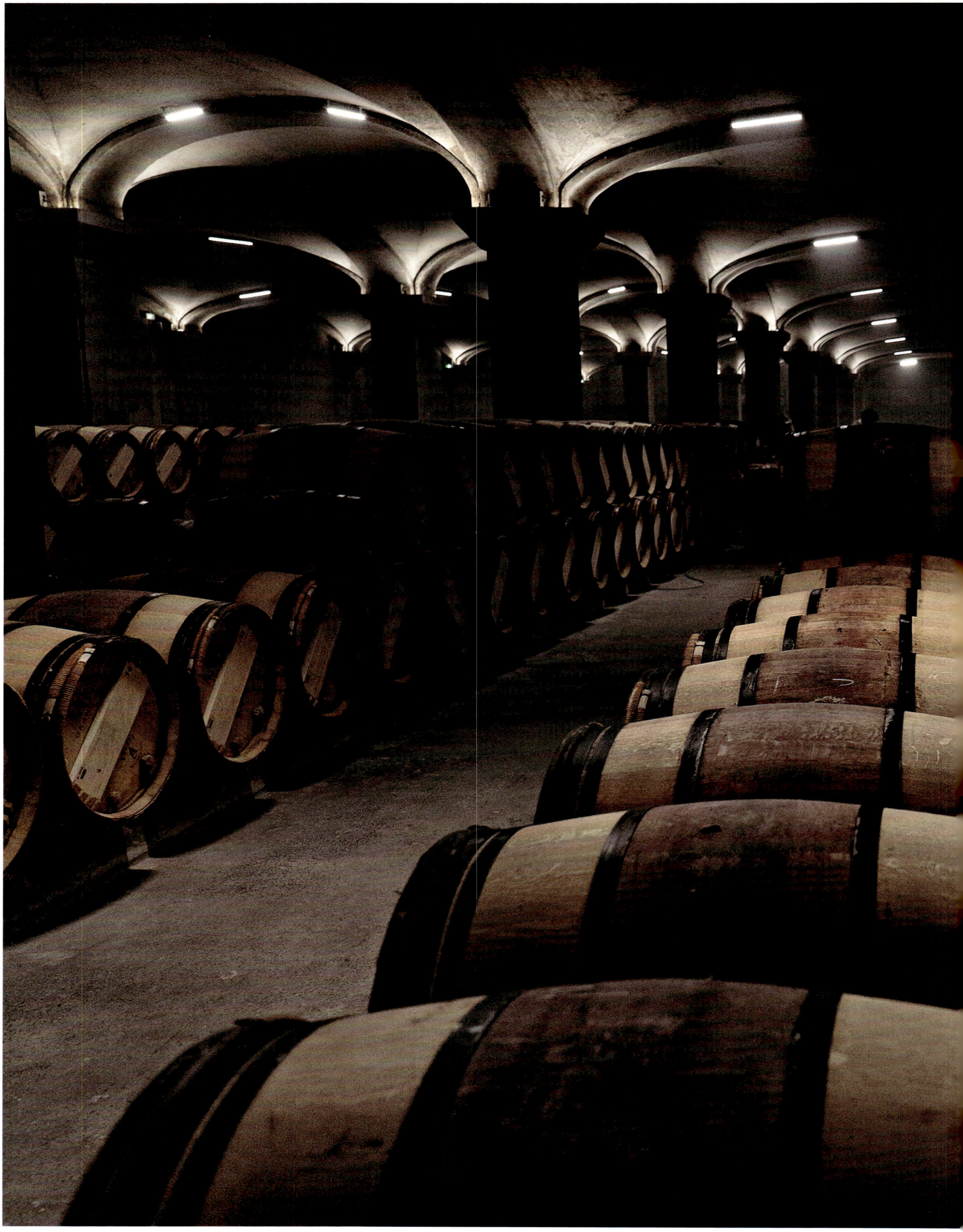

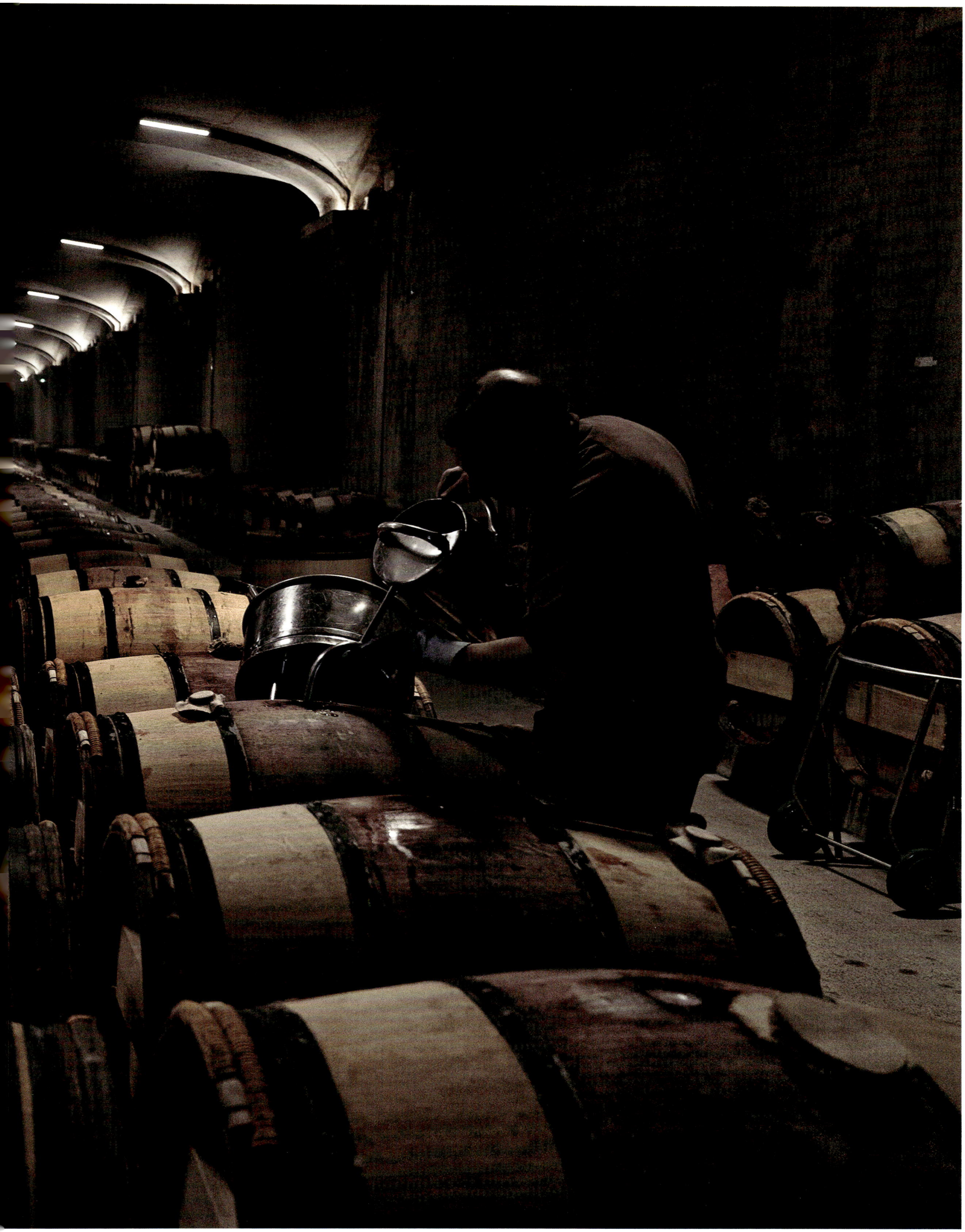

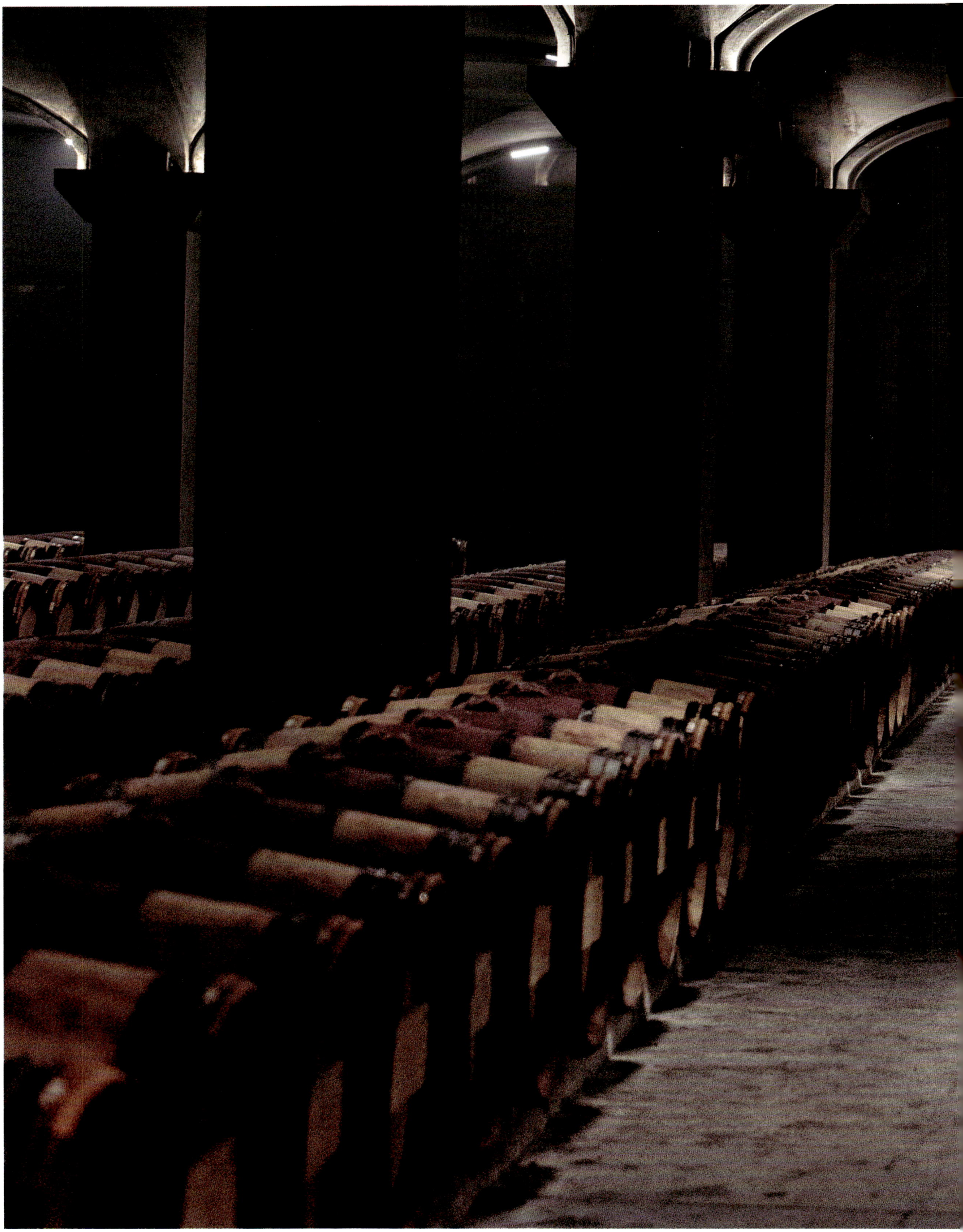

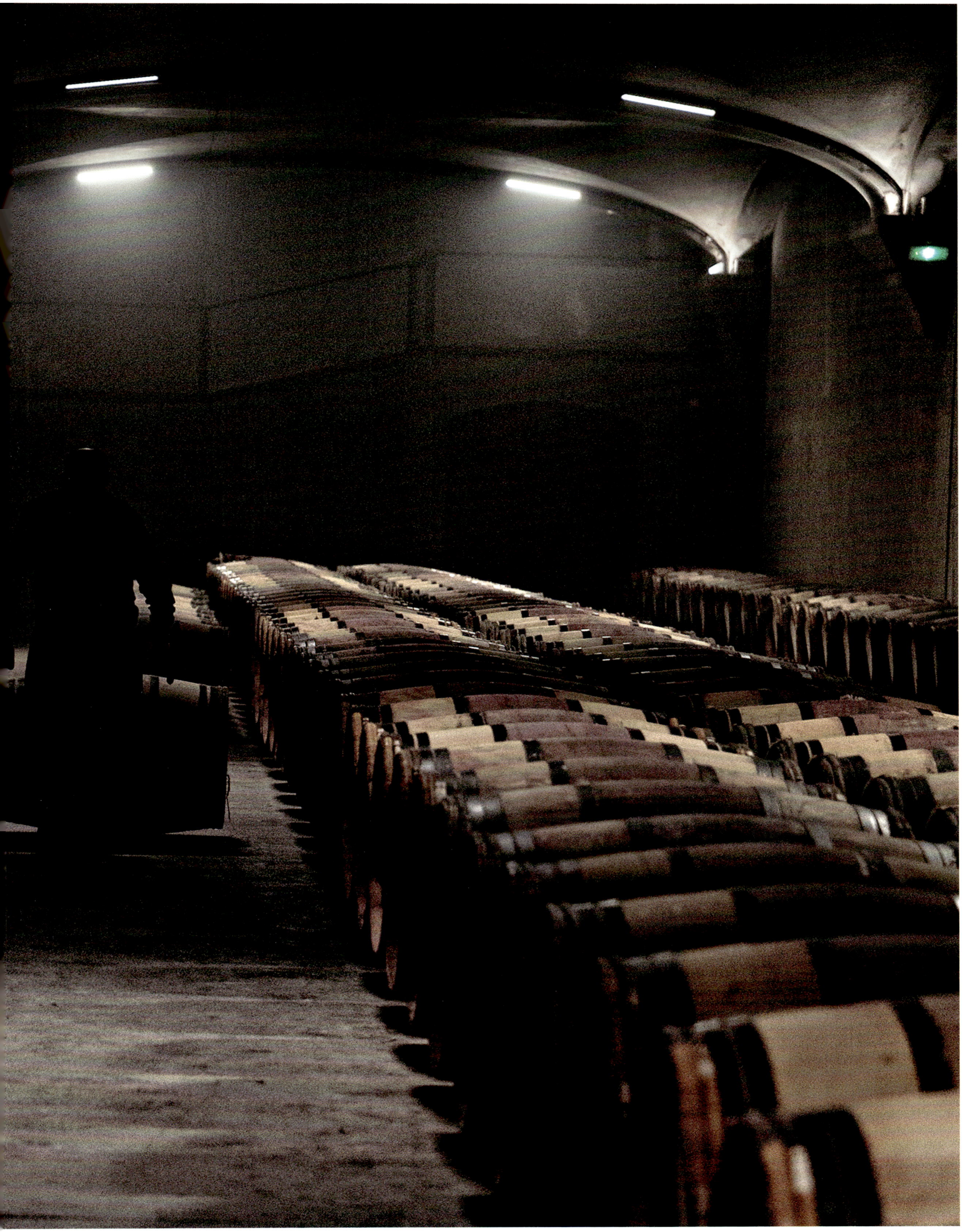

Ausone

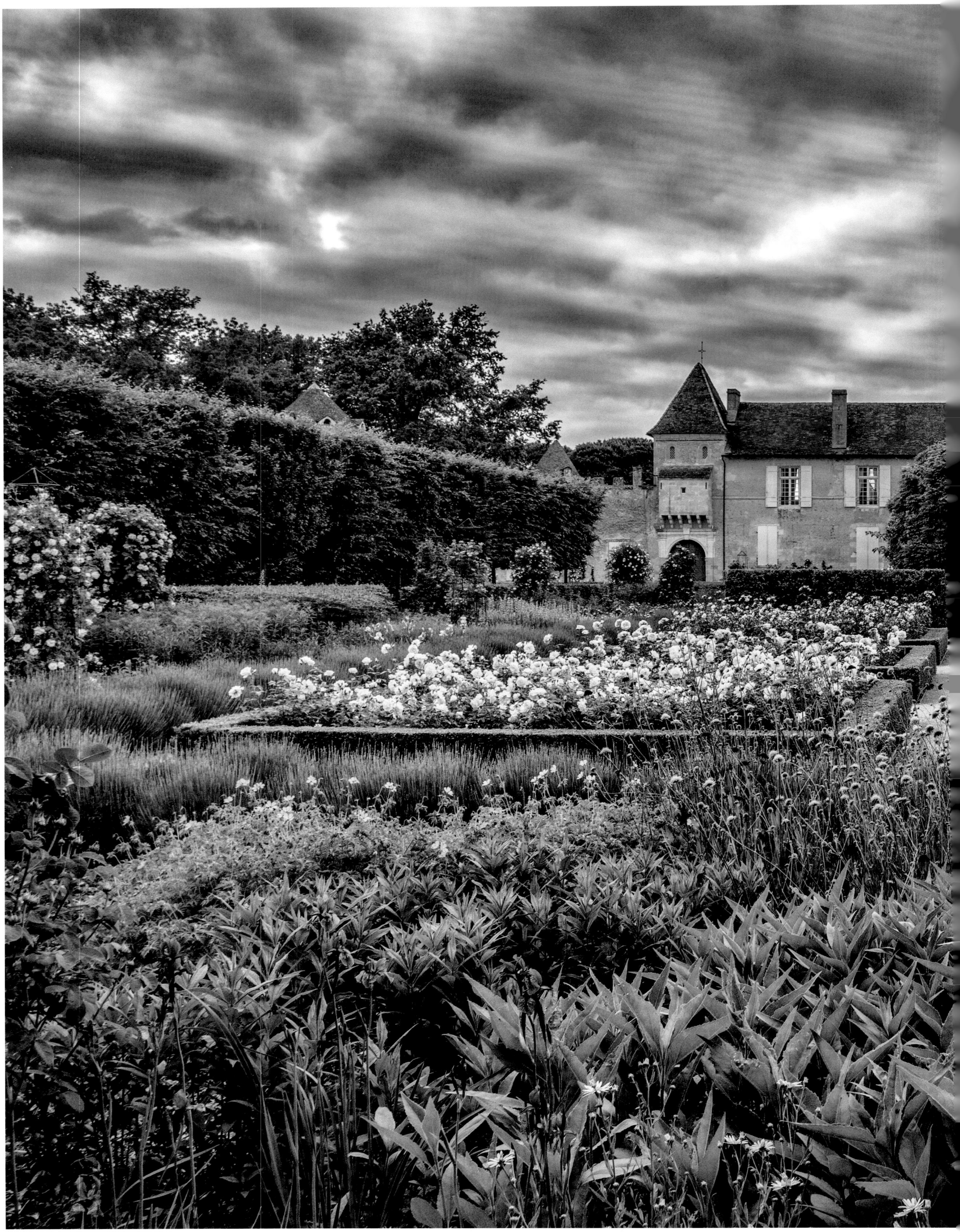

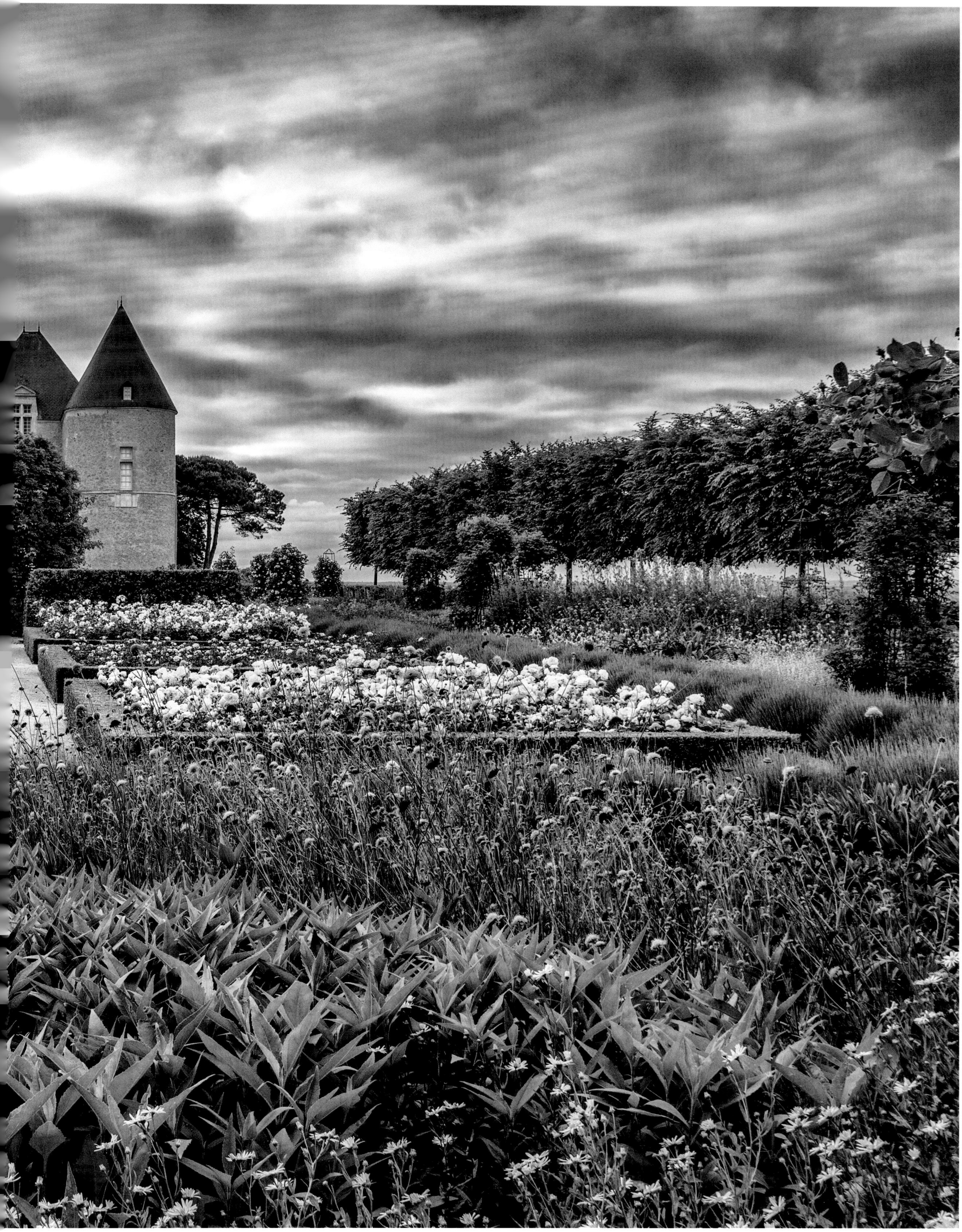

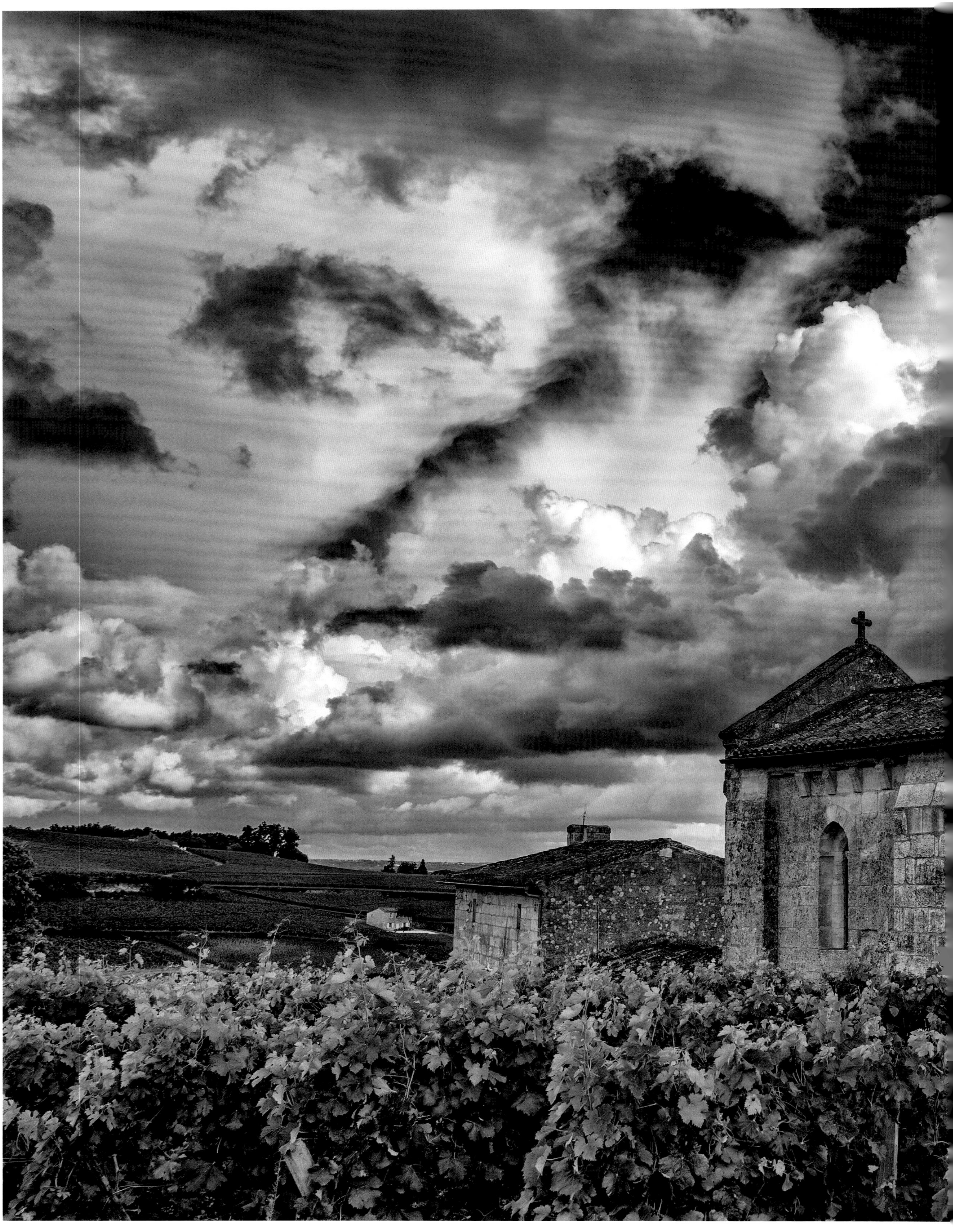

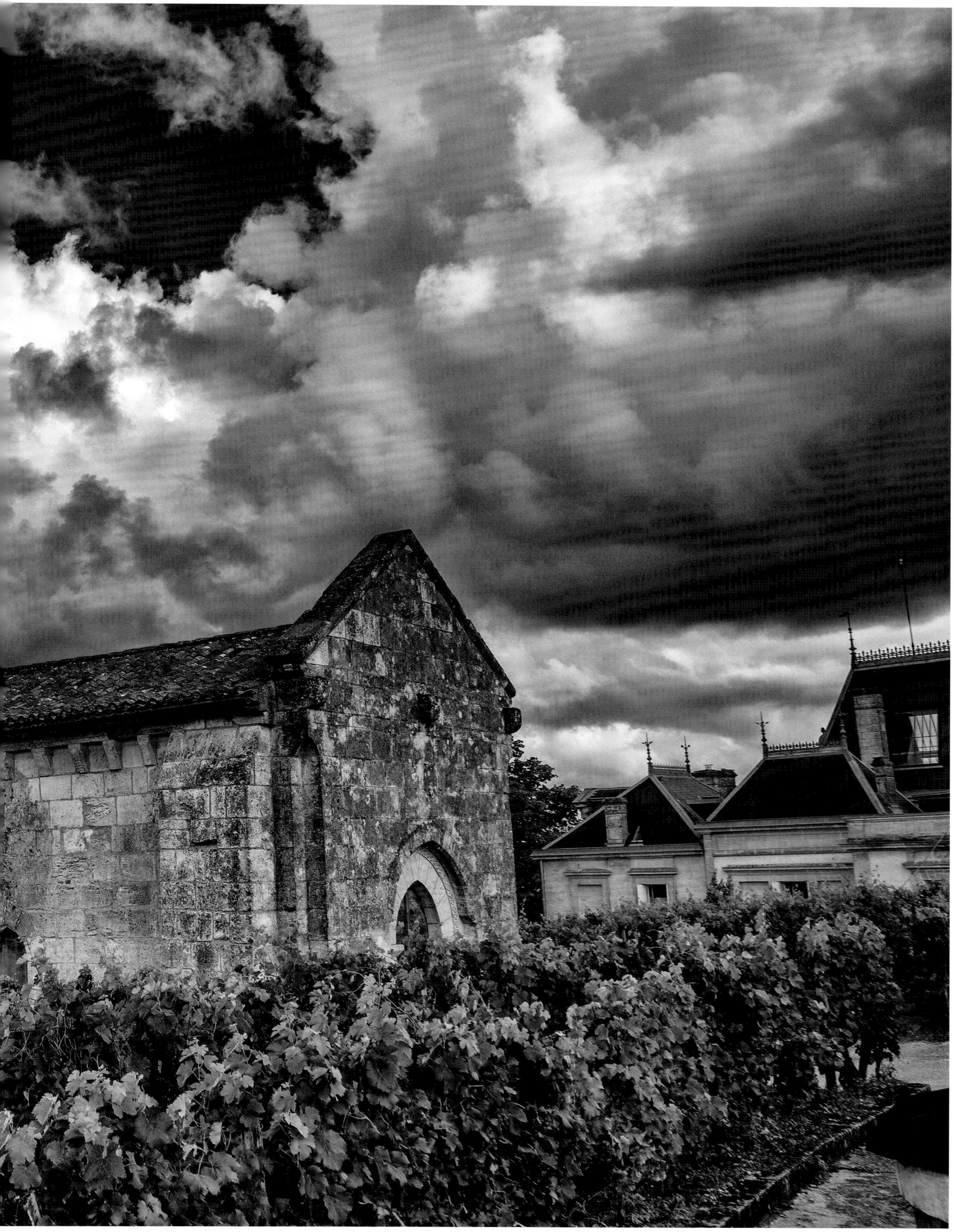

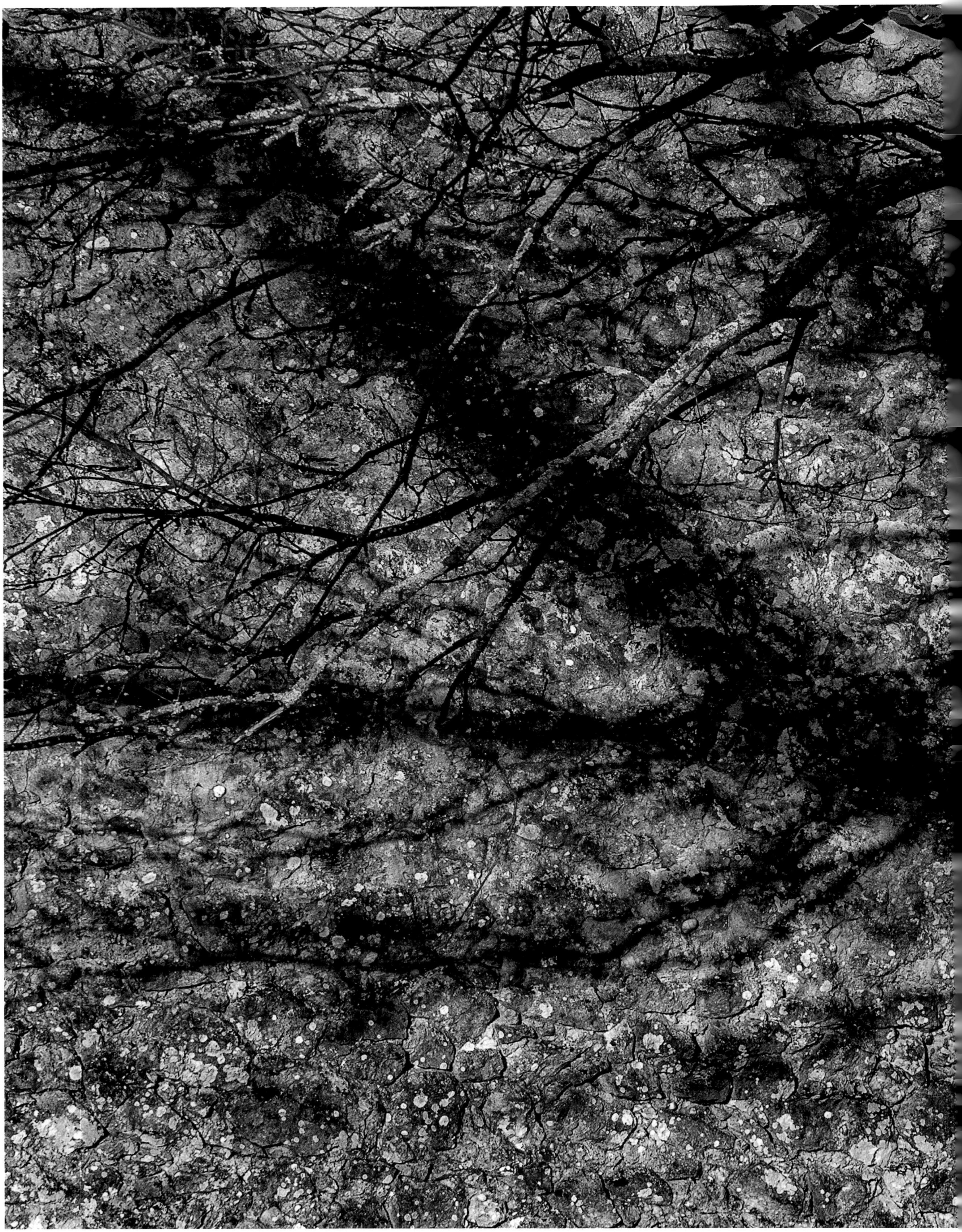

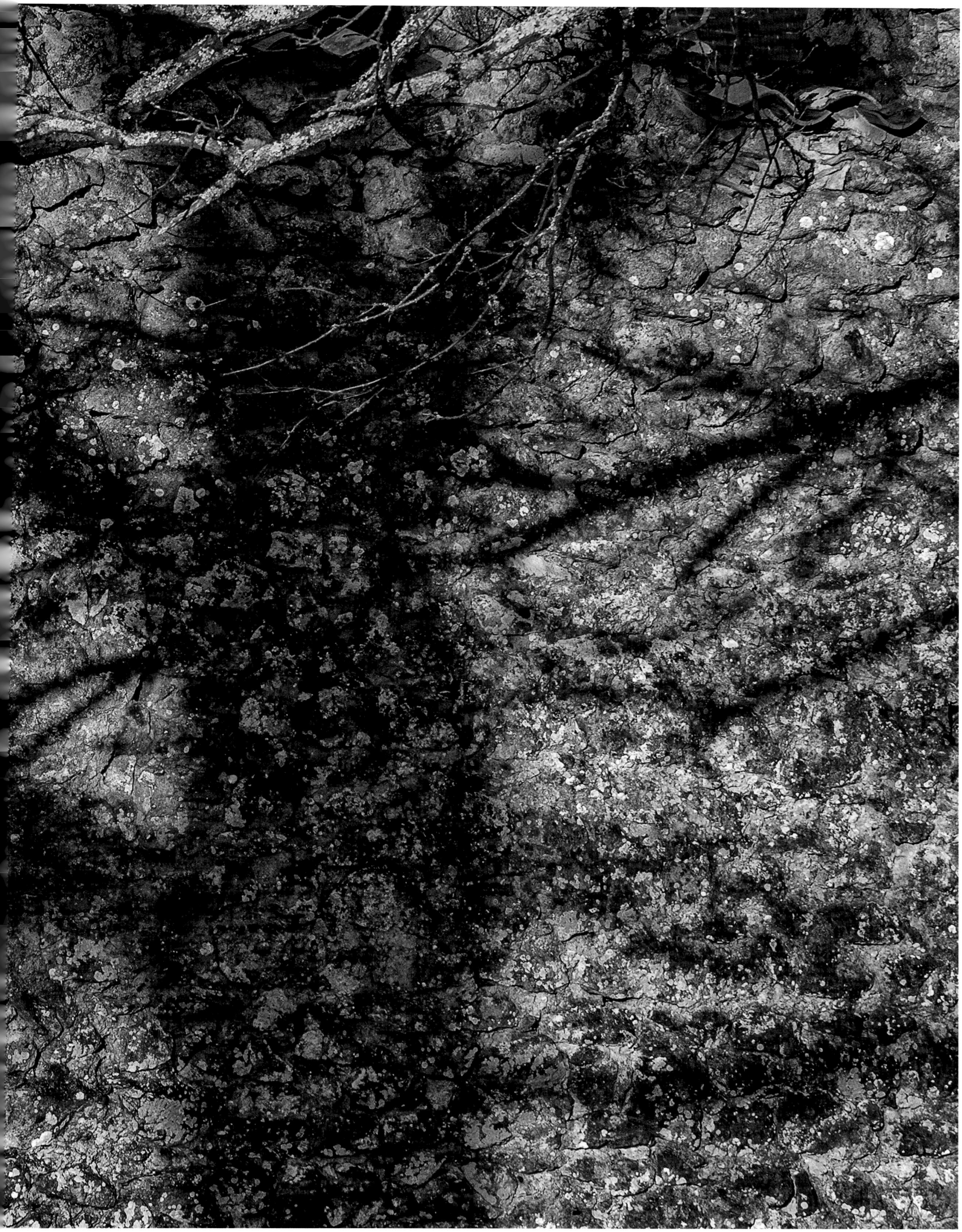

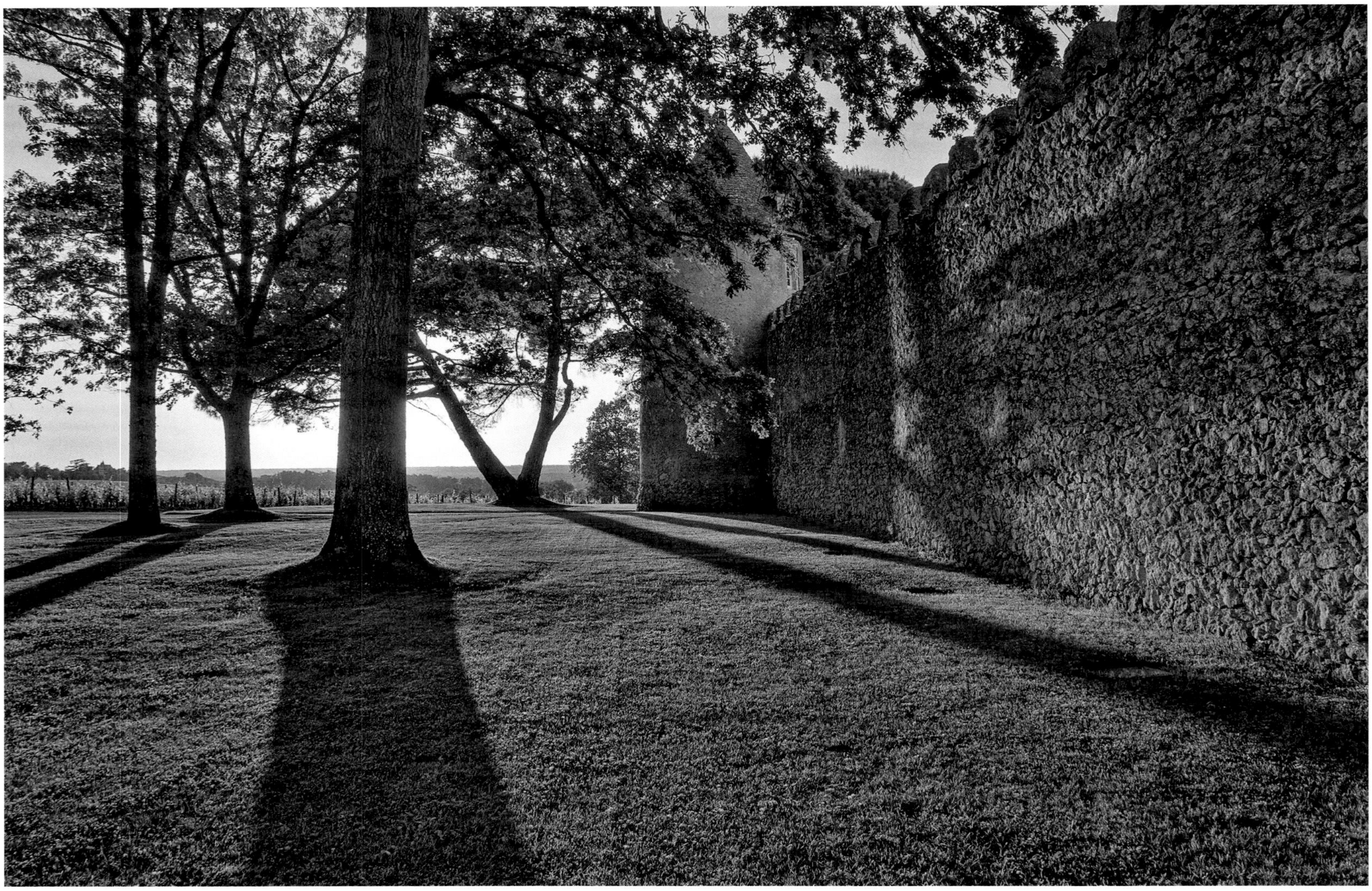

Yquem

Yquem

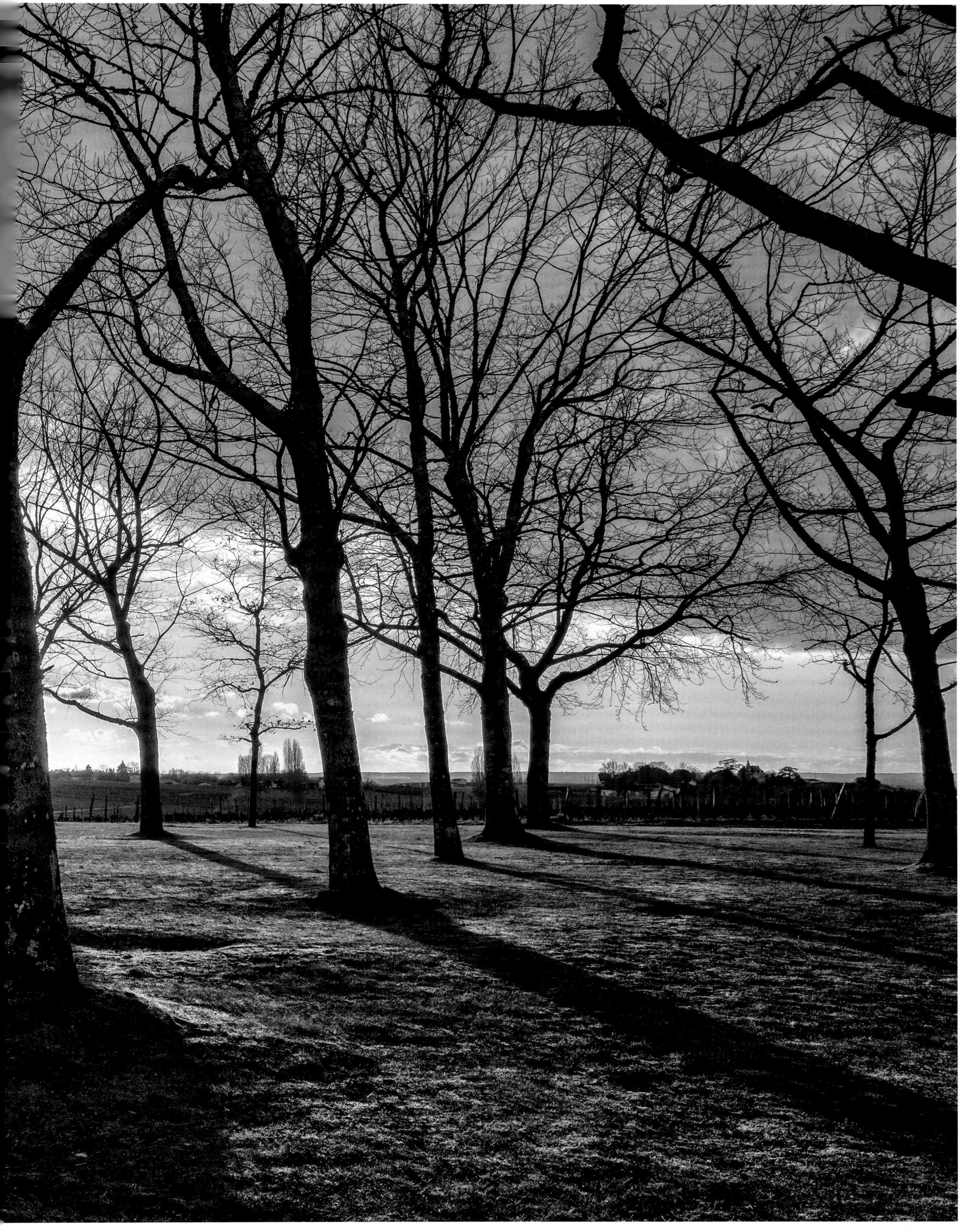

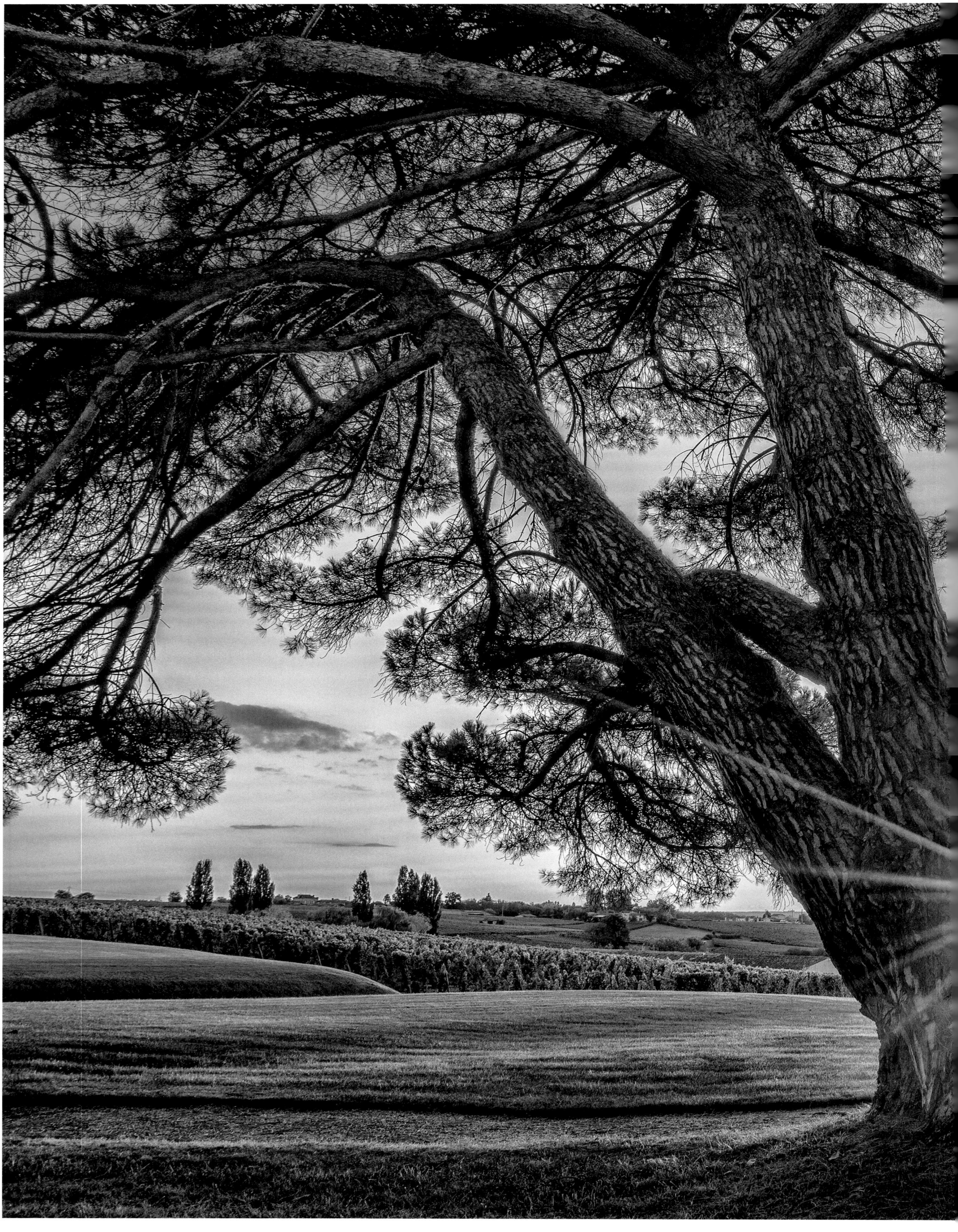

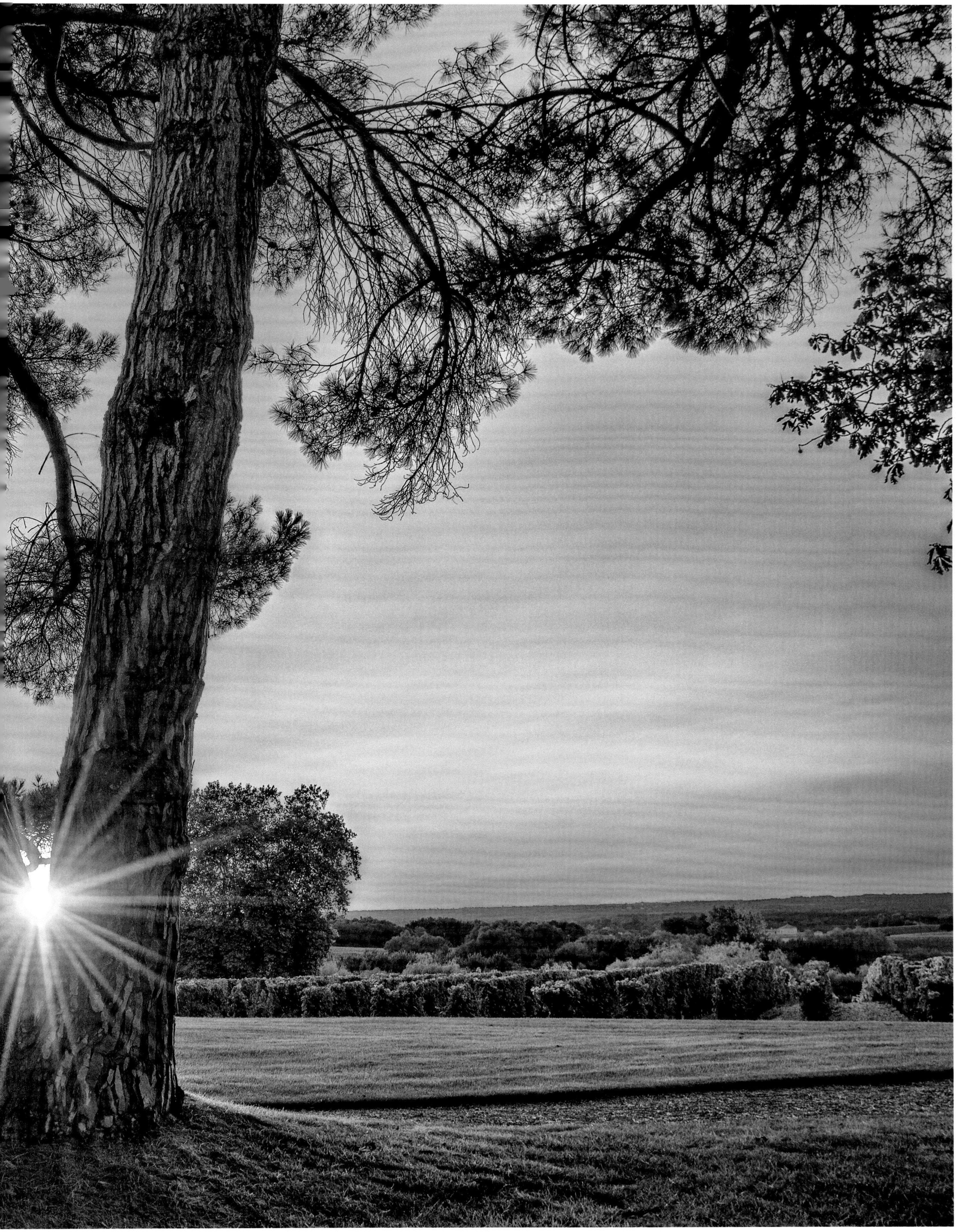

Margaux

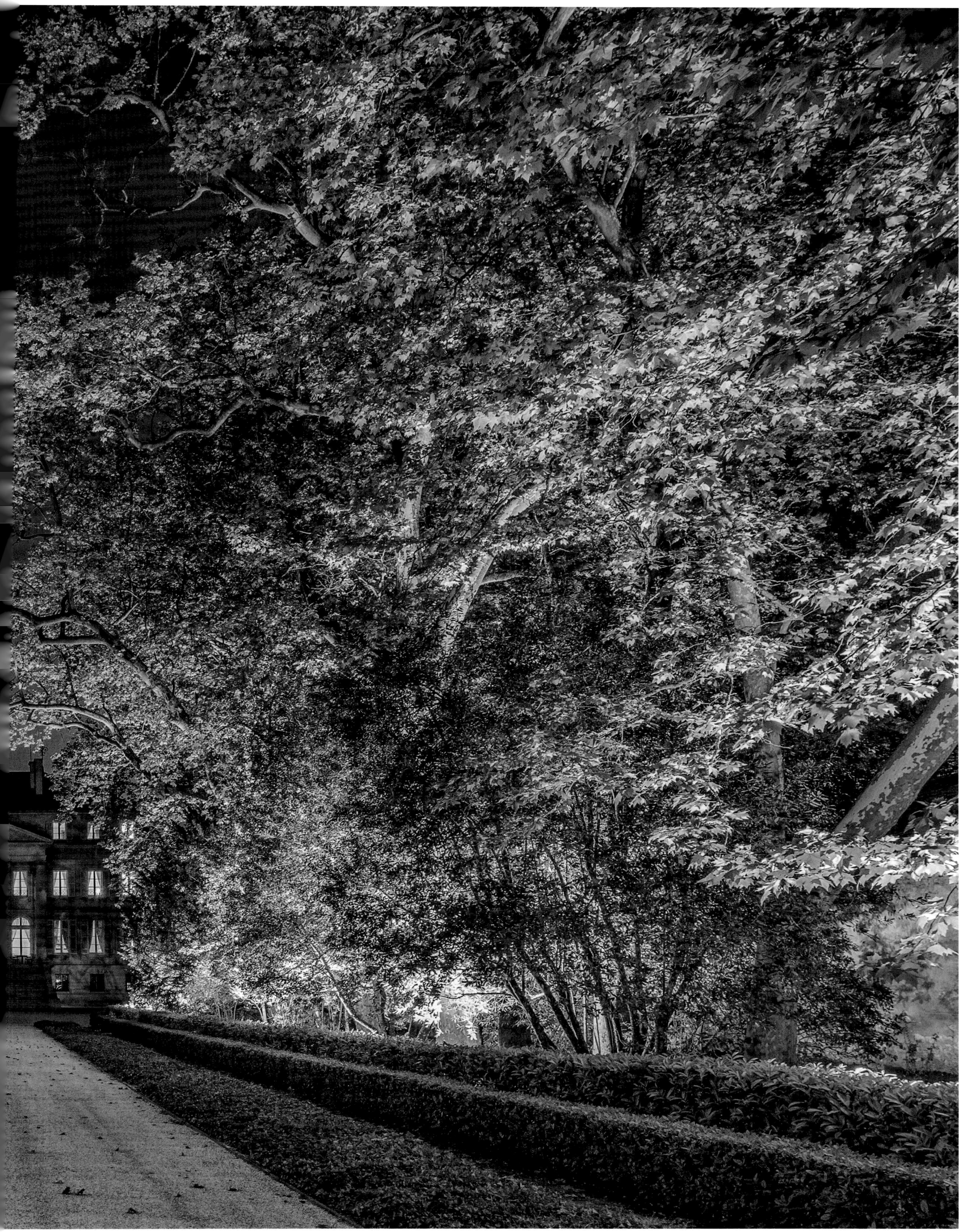

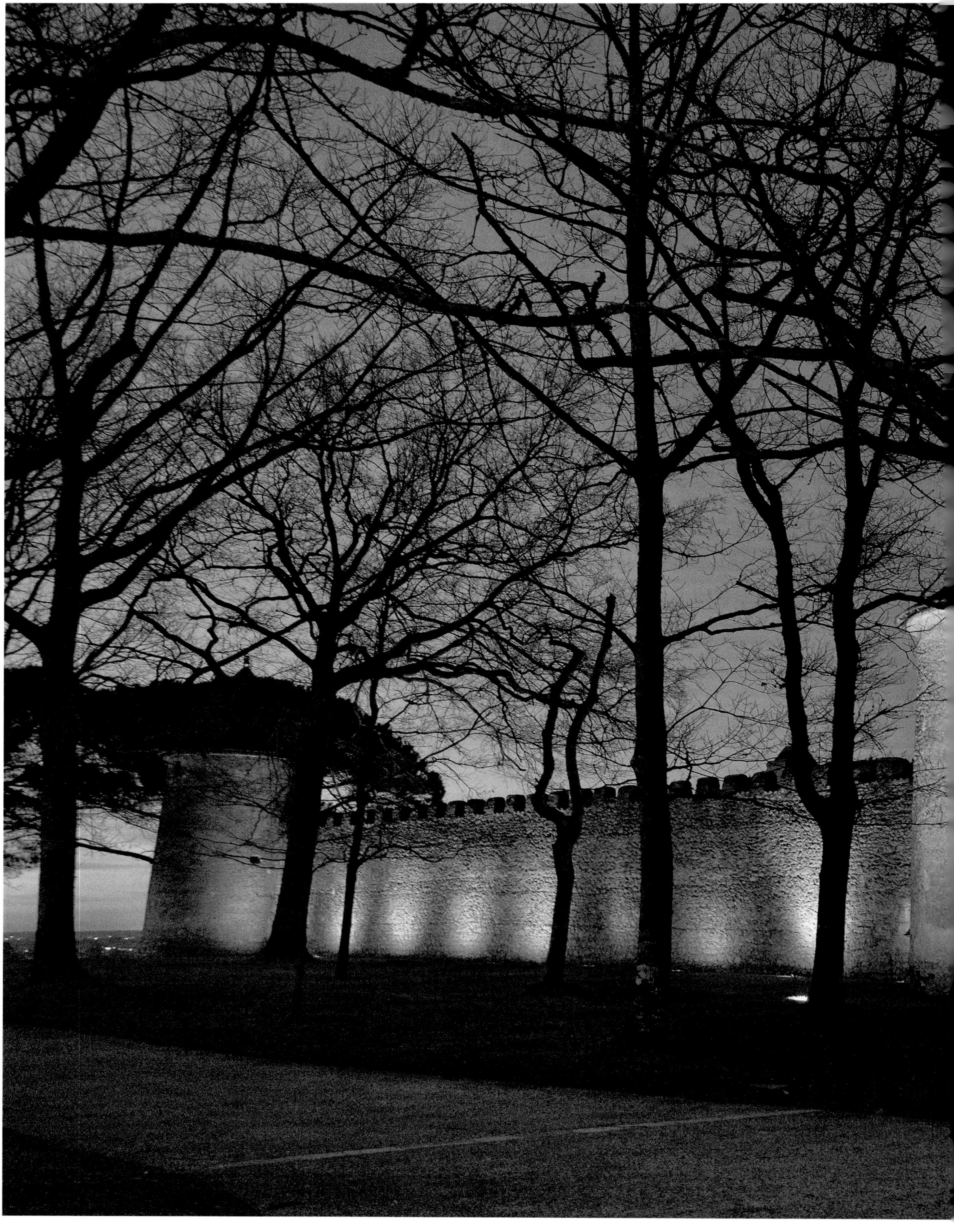

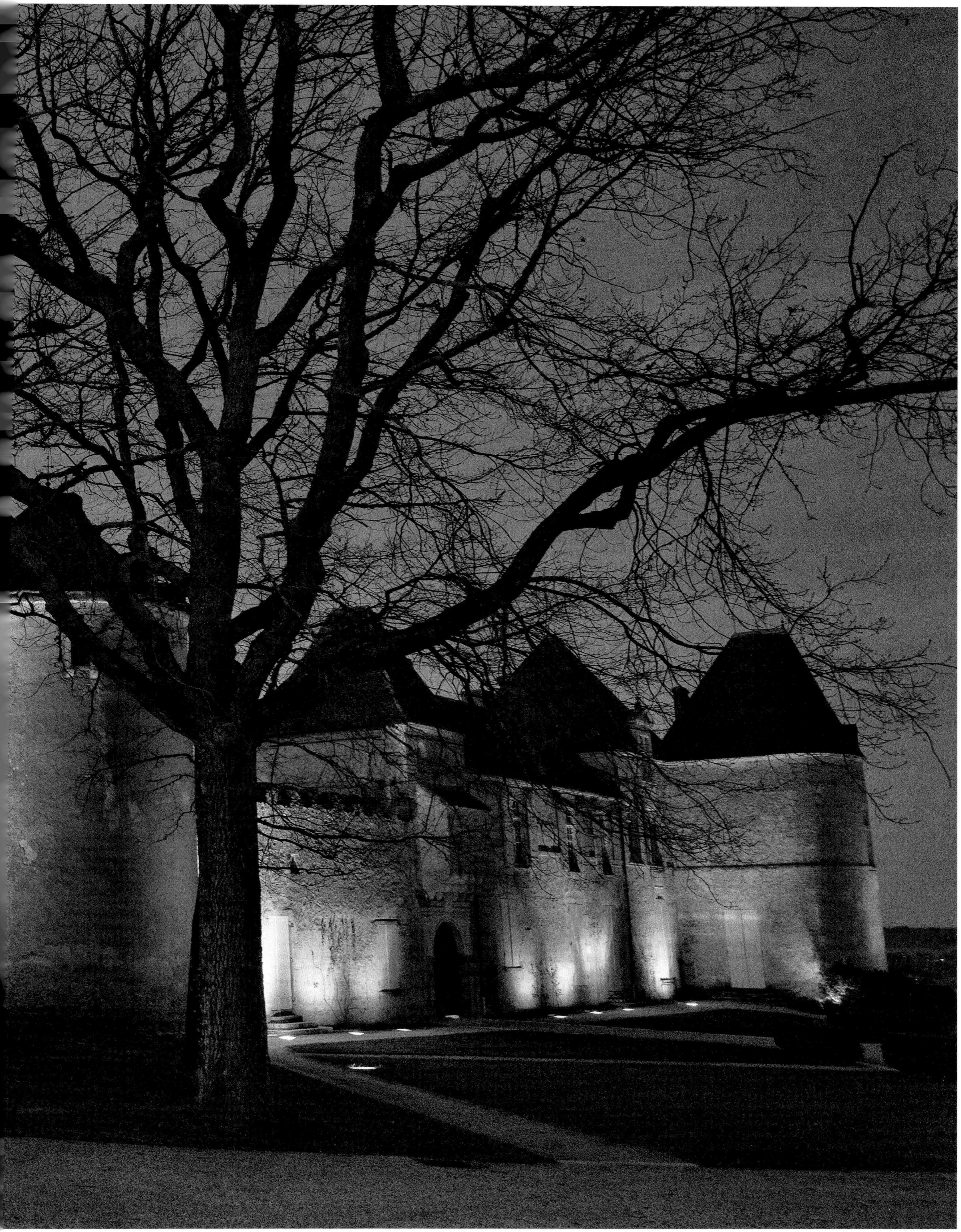

Mouton

Cheval Blanc

83

Cheval Blanc

Cheval Blanc

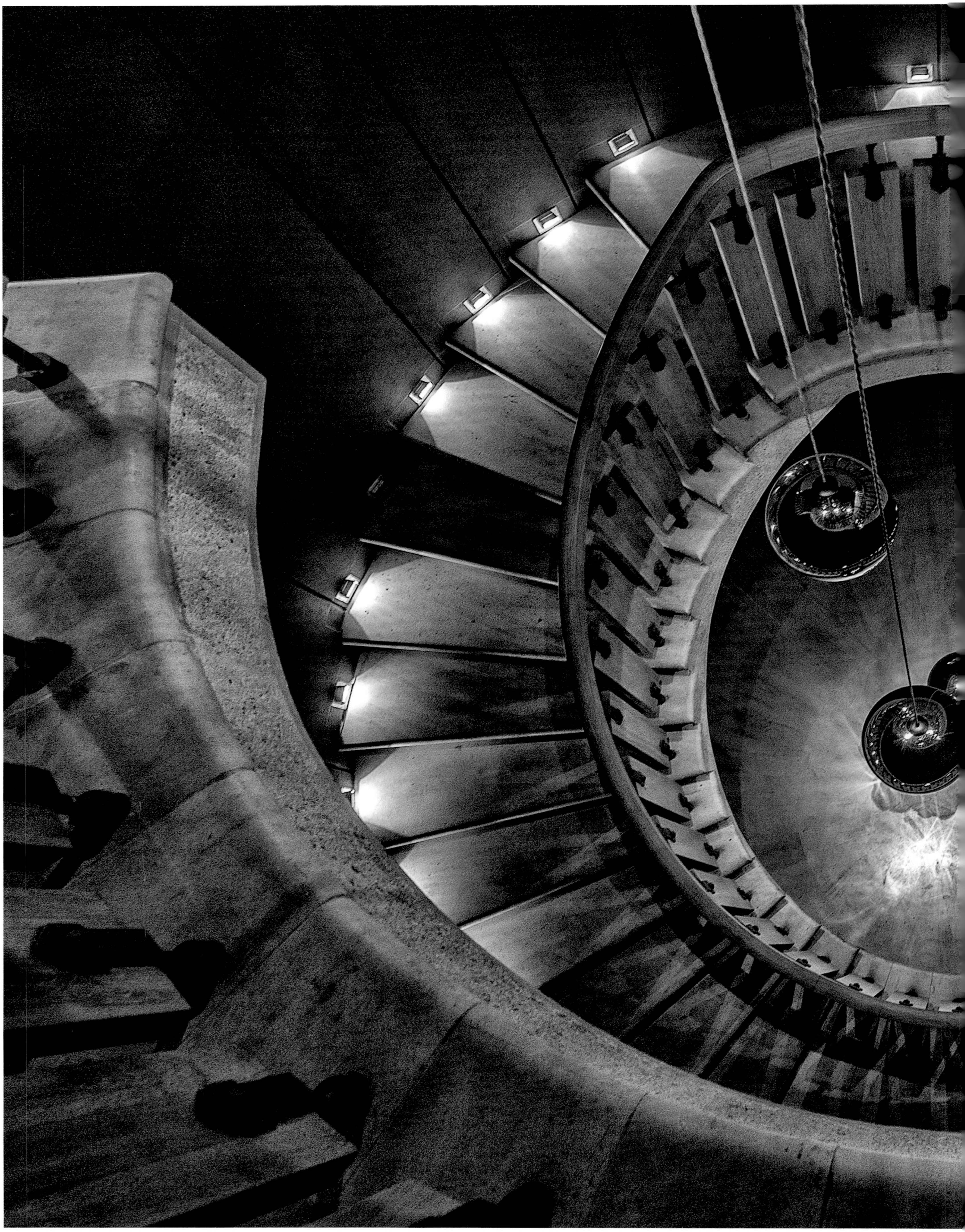

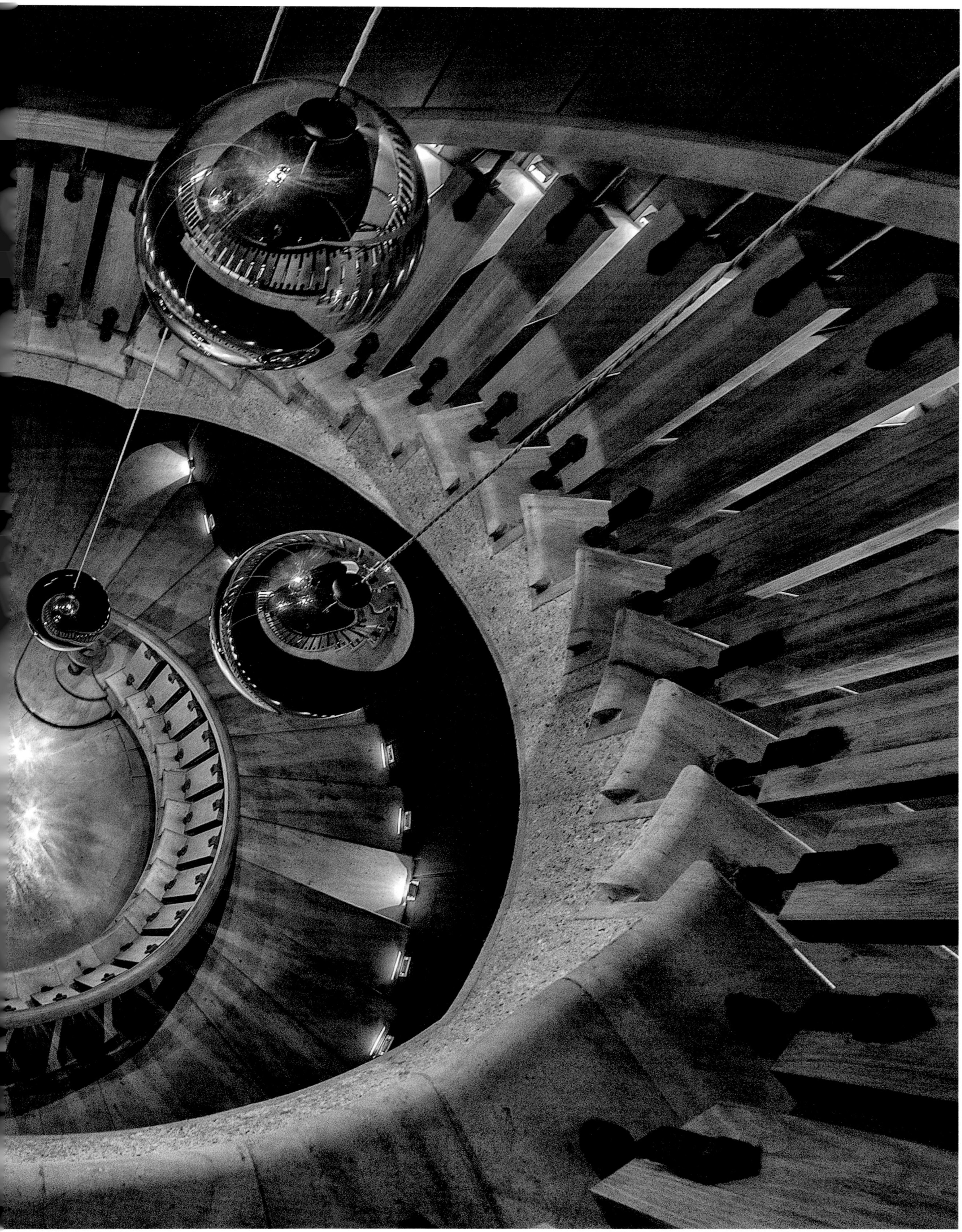

88   Latour

89

90 Mouton

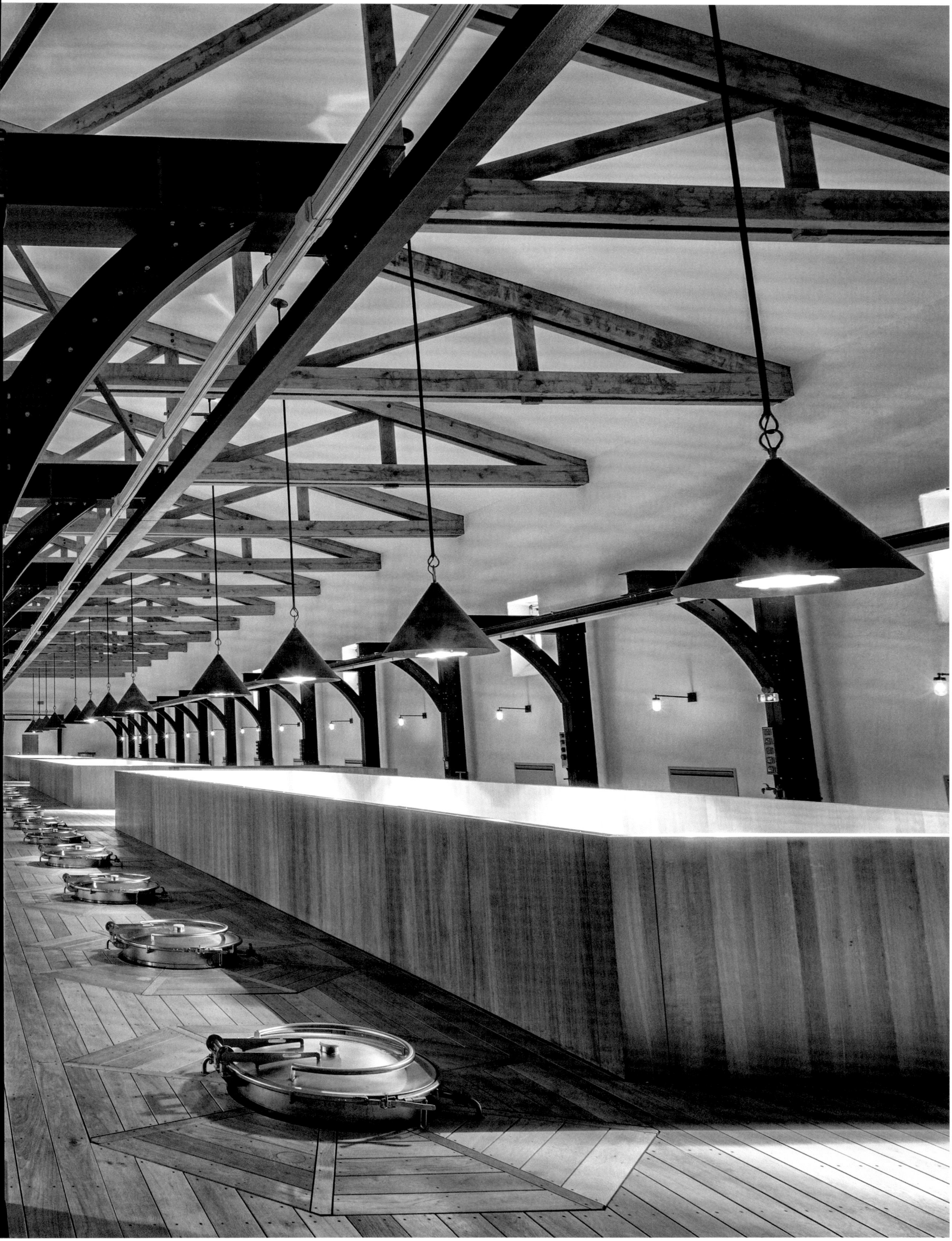

Ausone

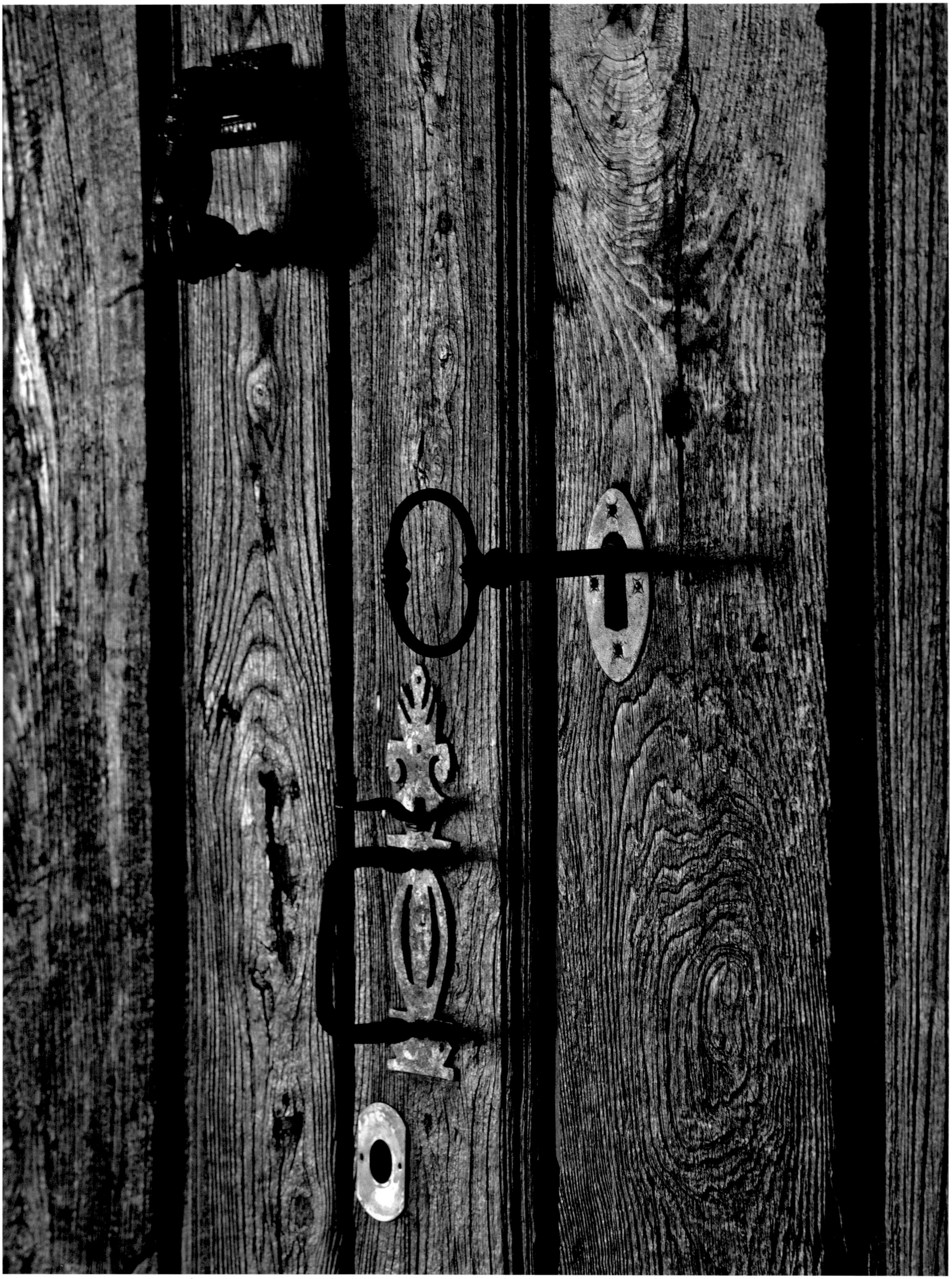

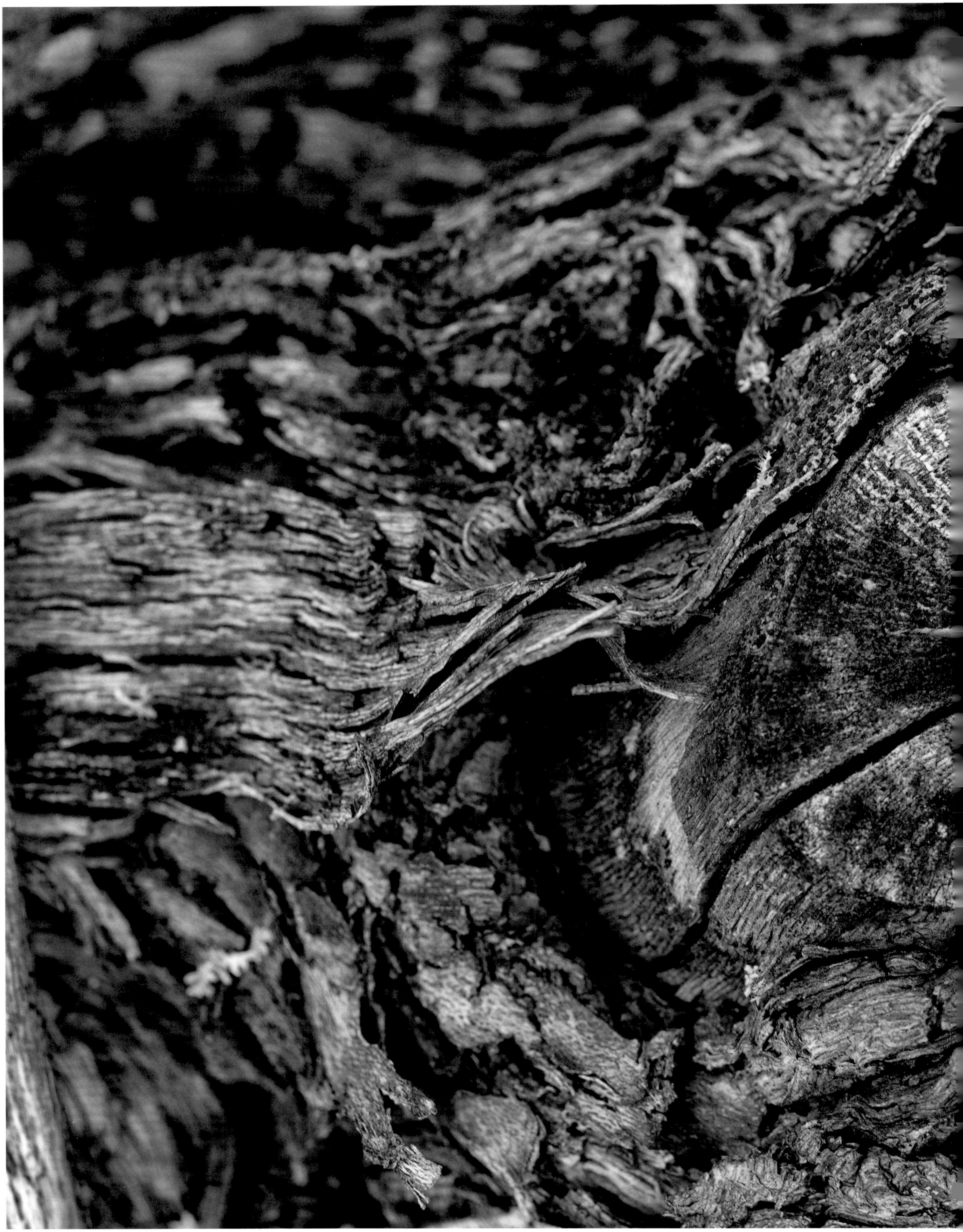

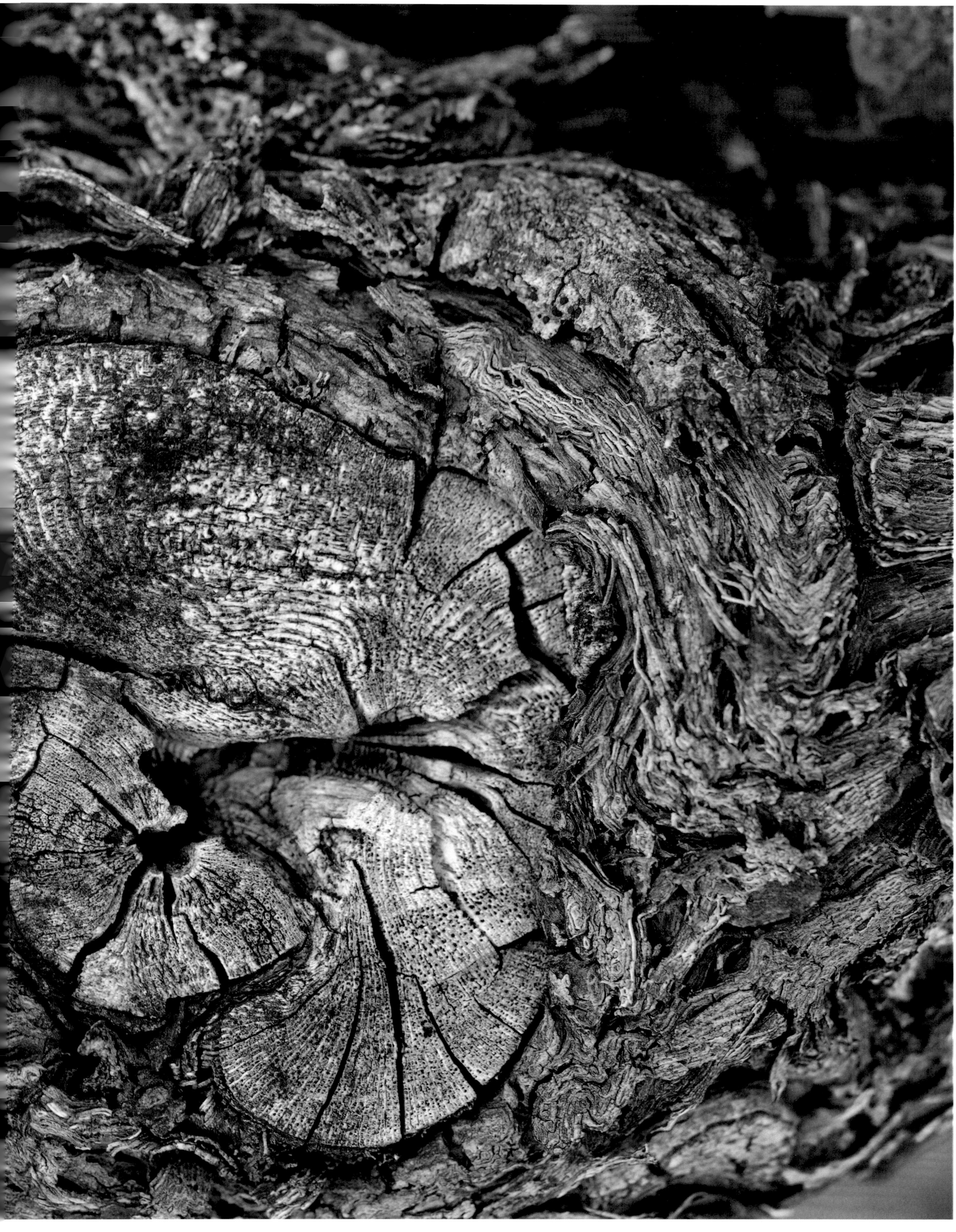

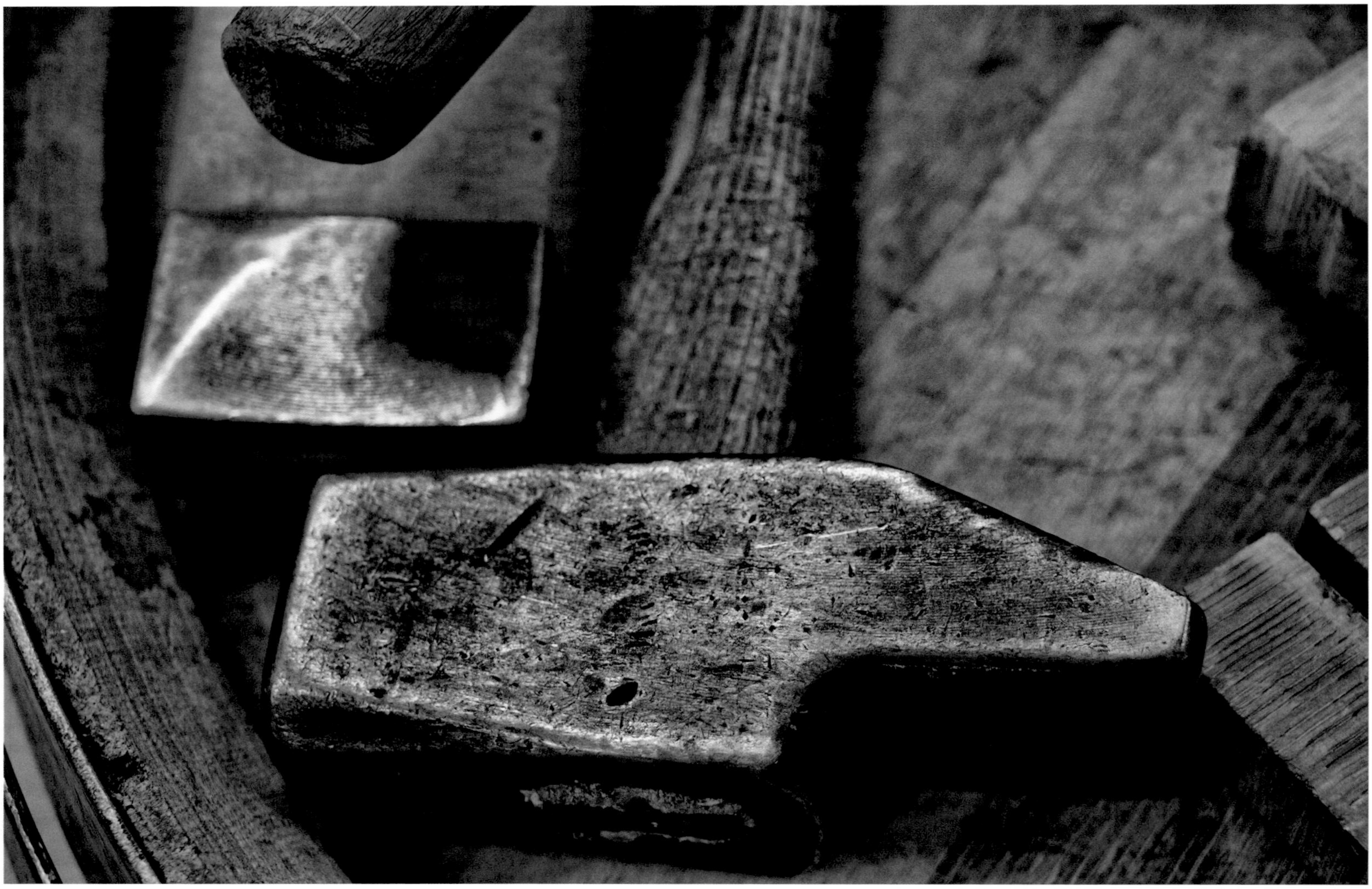

Margaux

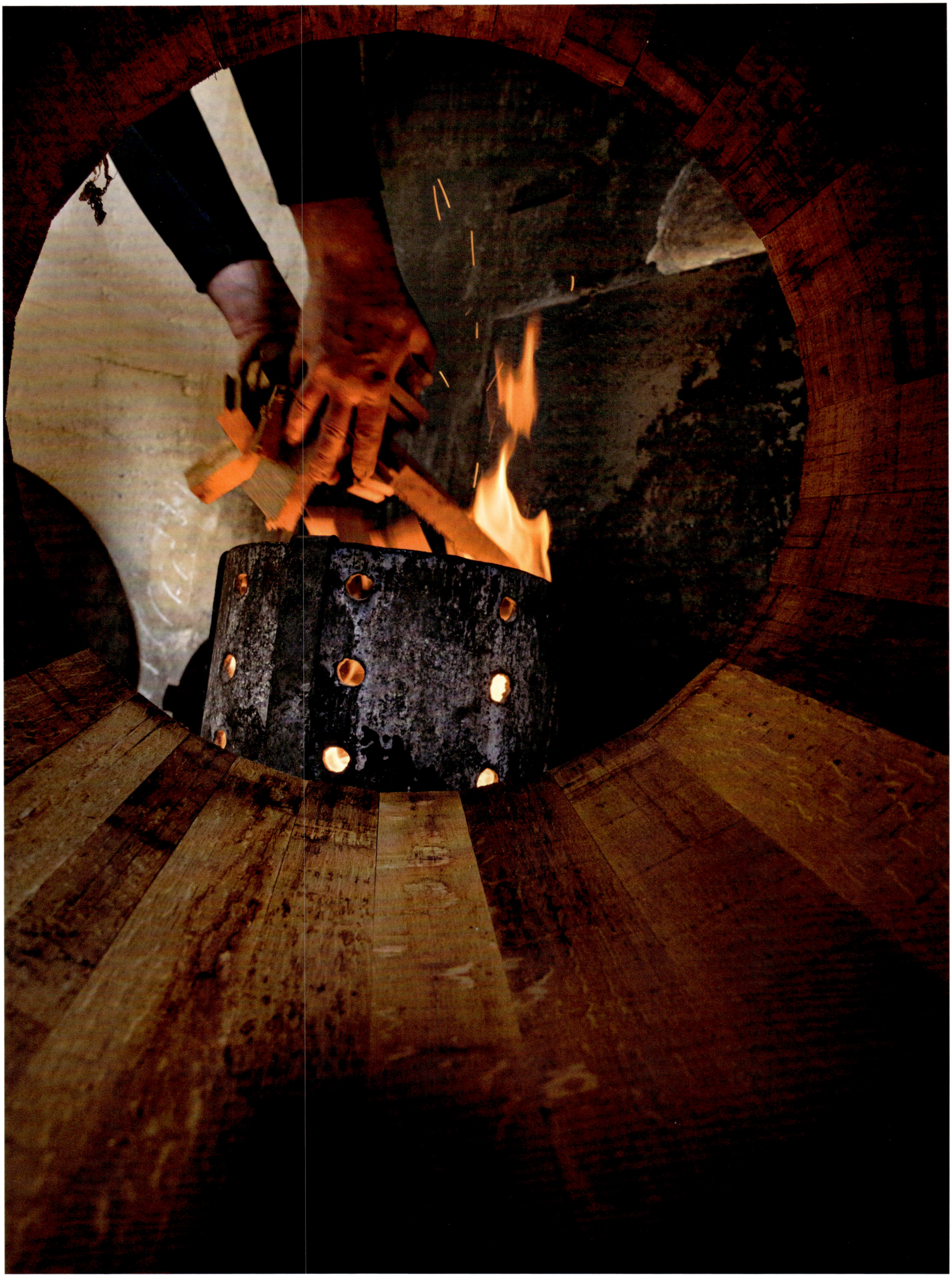

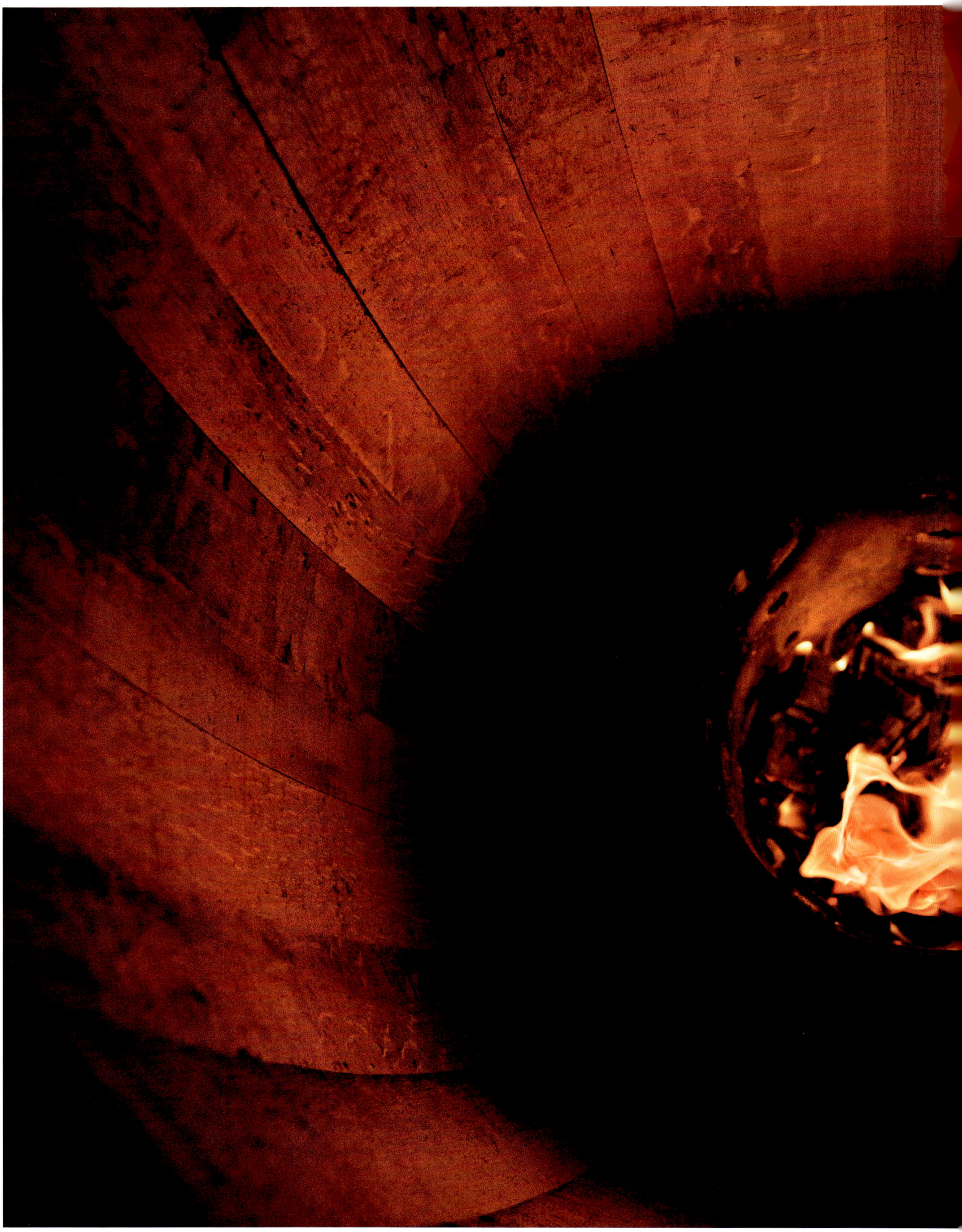

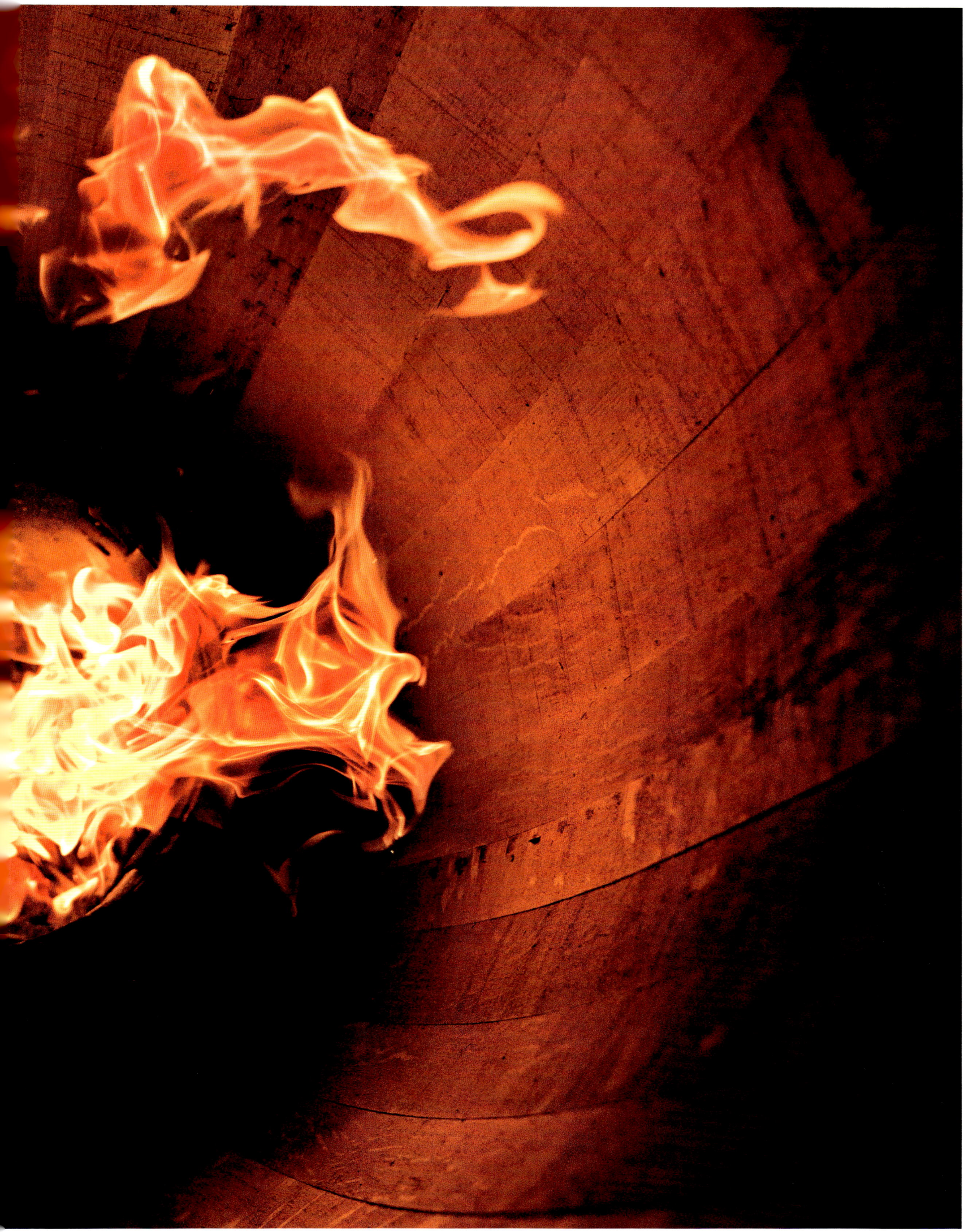

Margaux

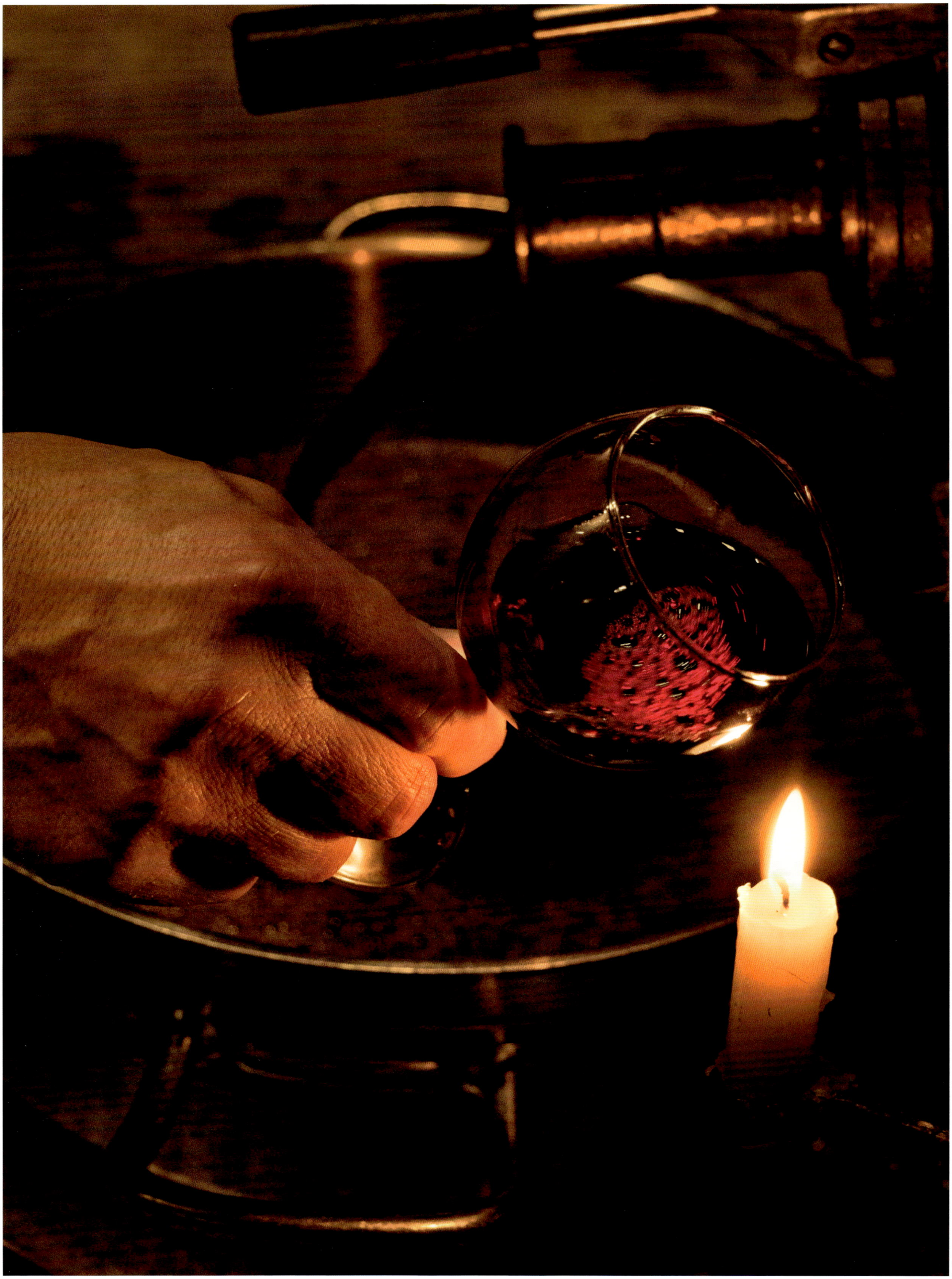

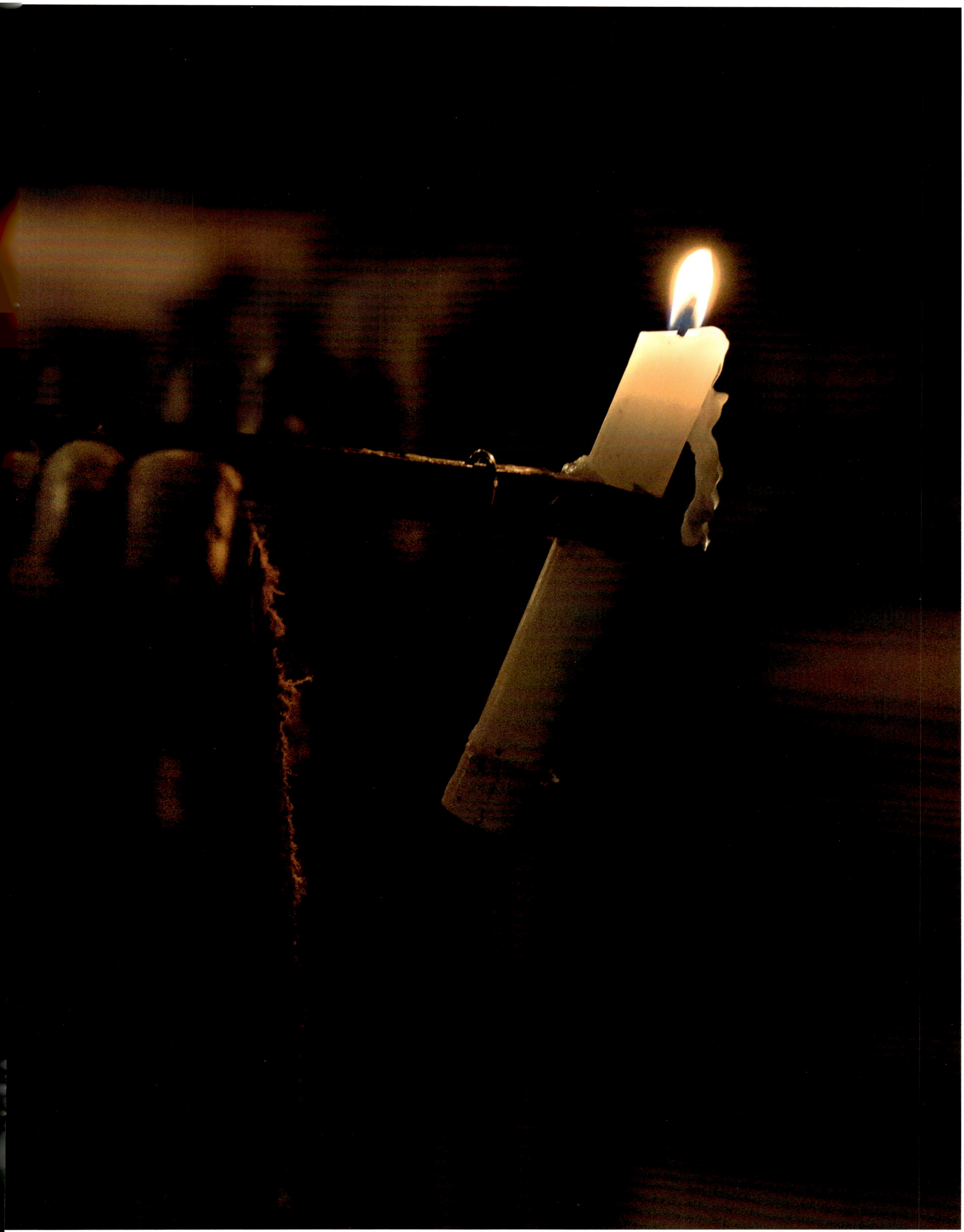

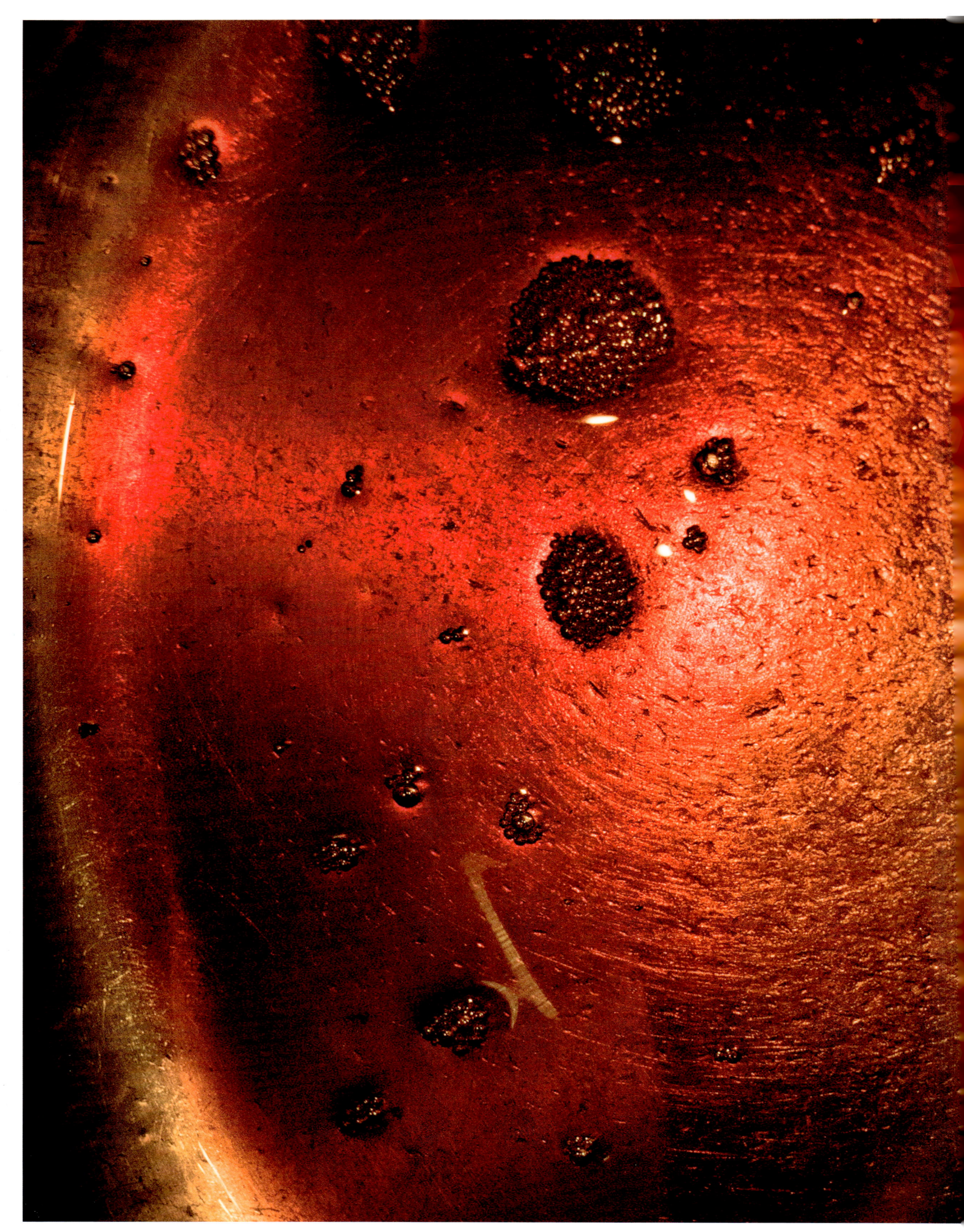

Haut-Brion

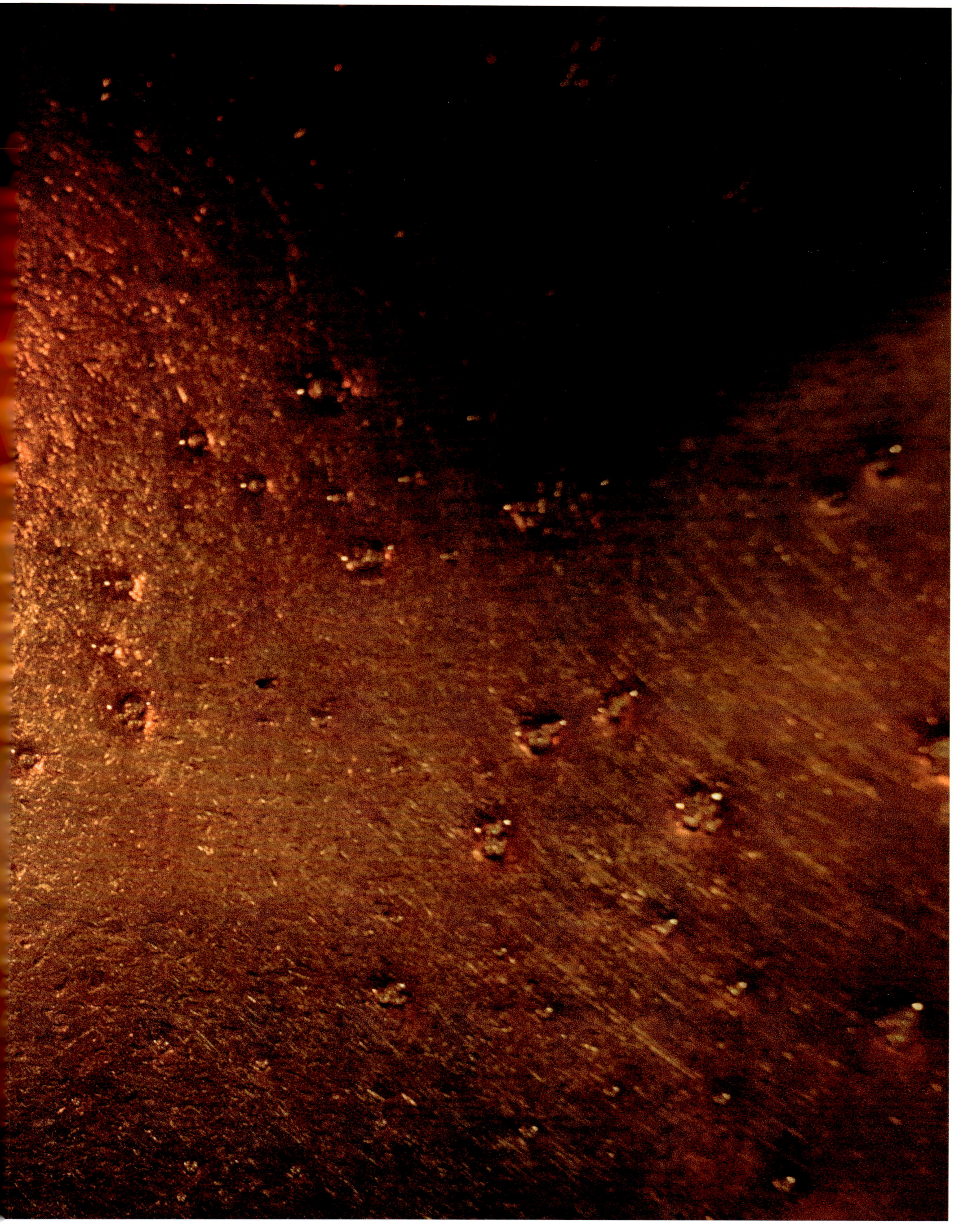

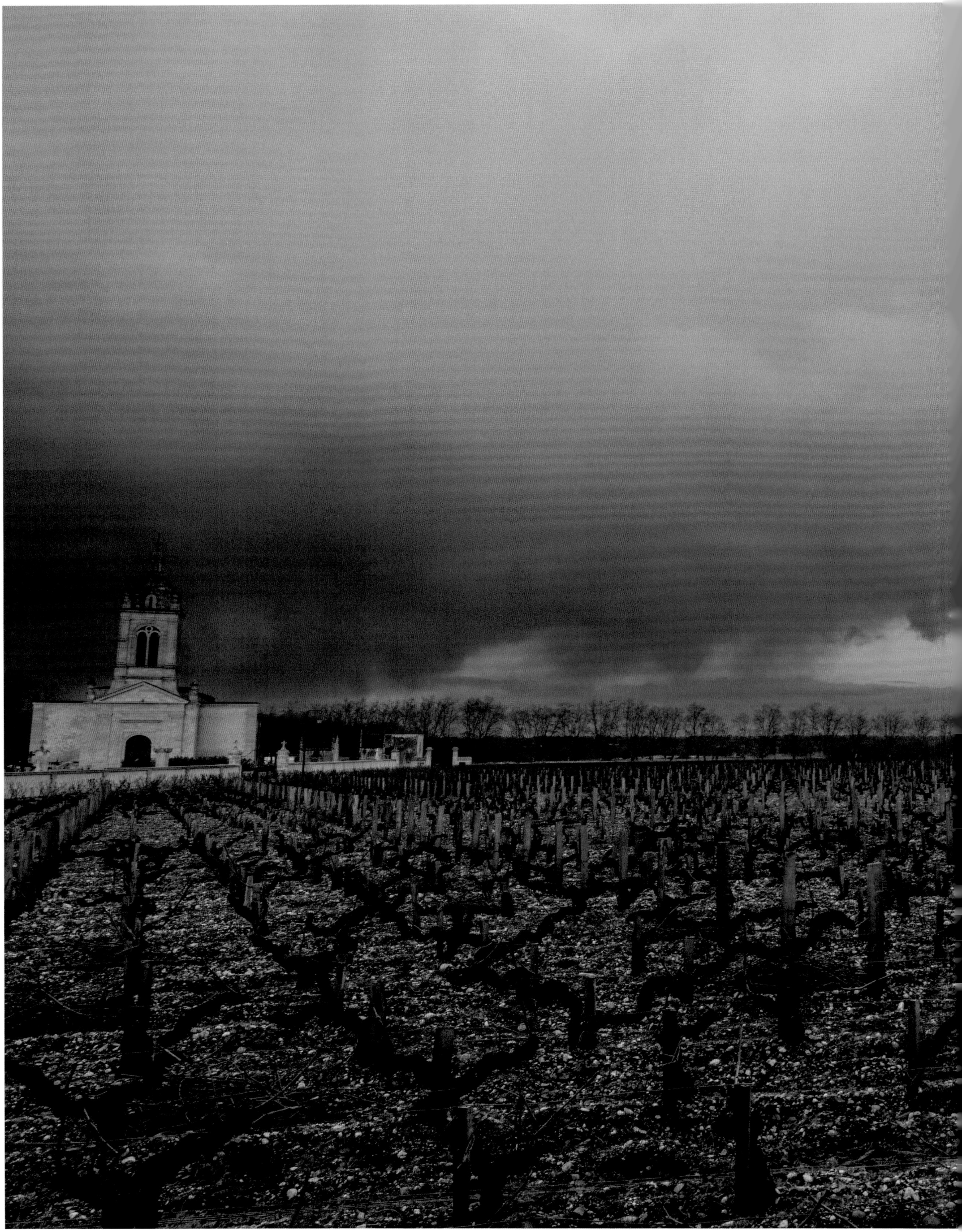

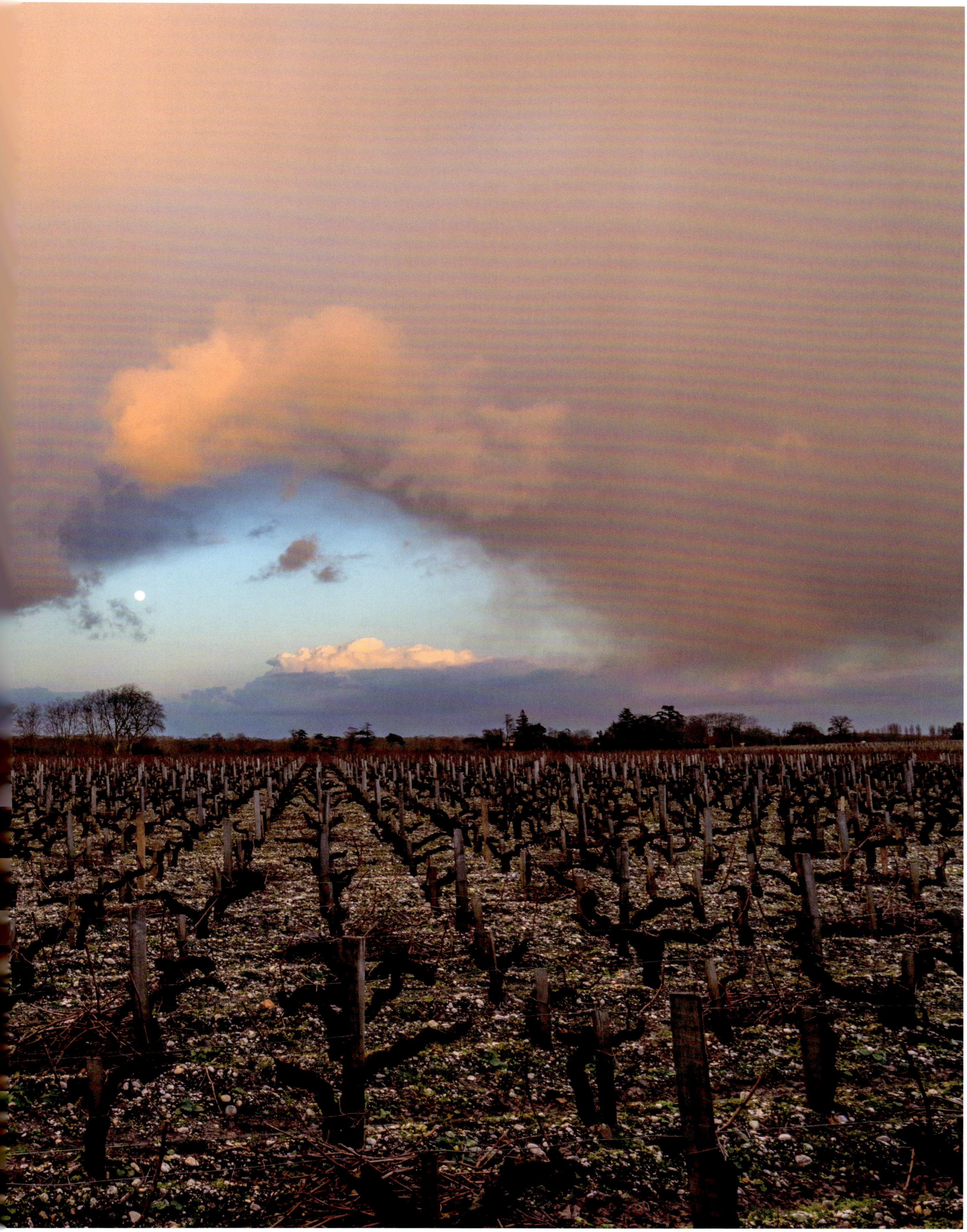

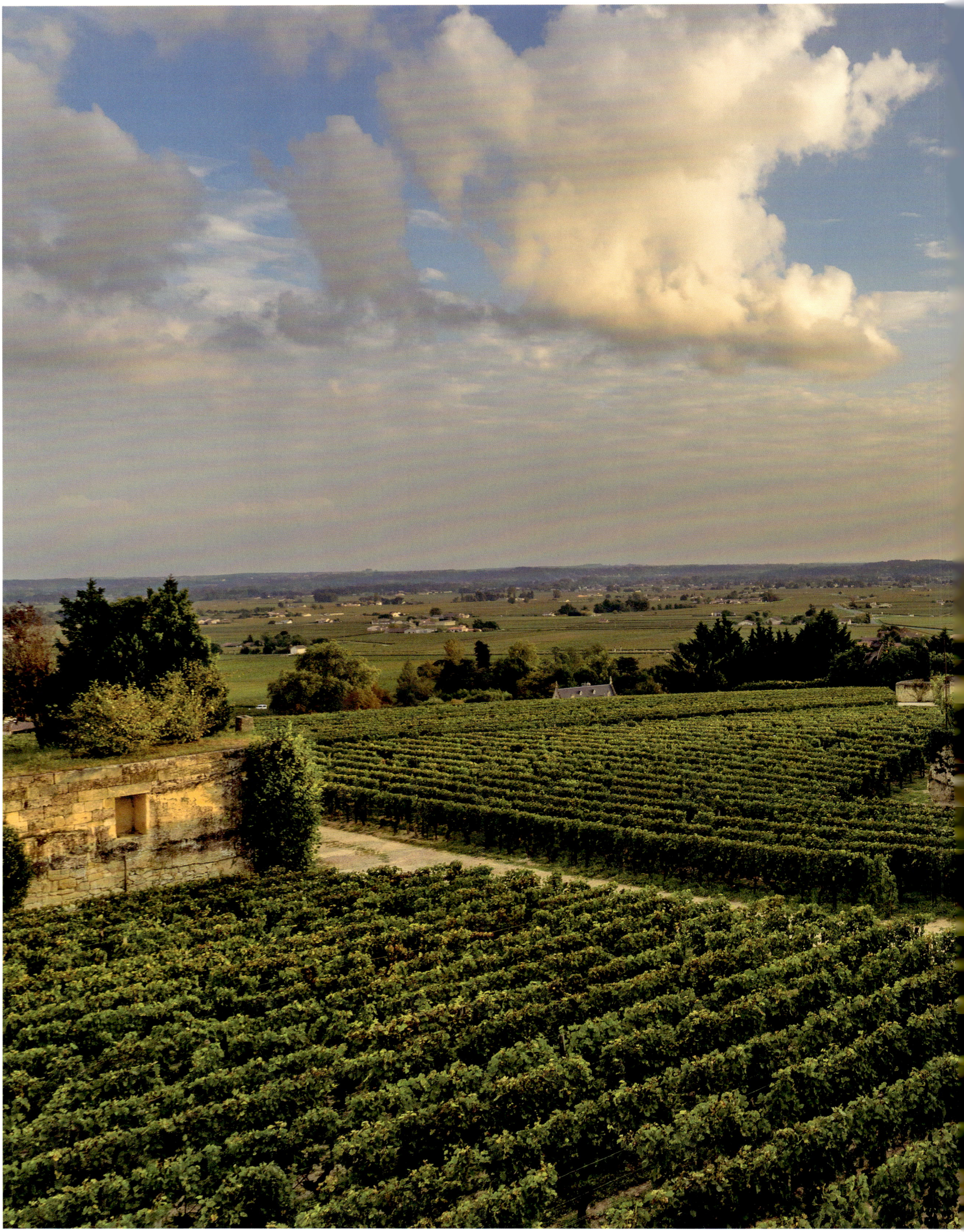

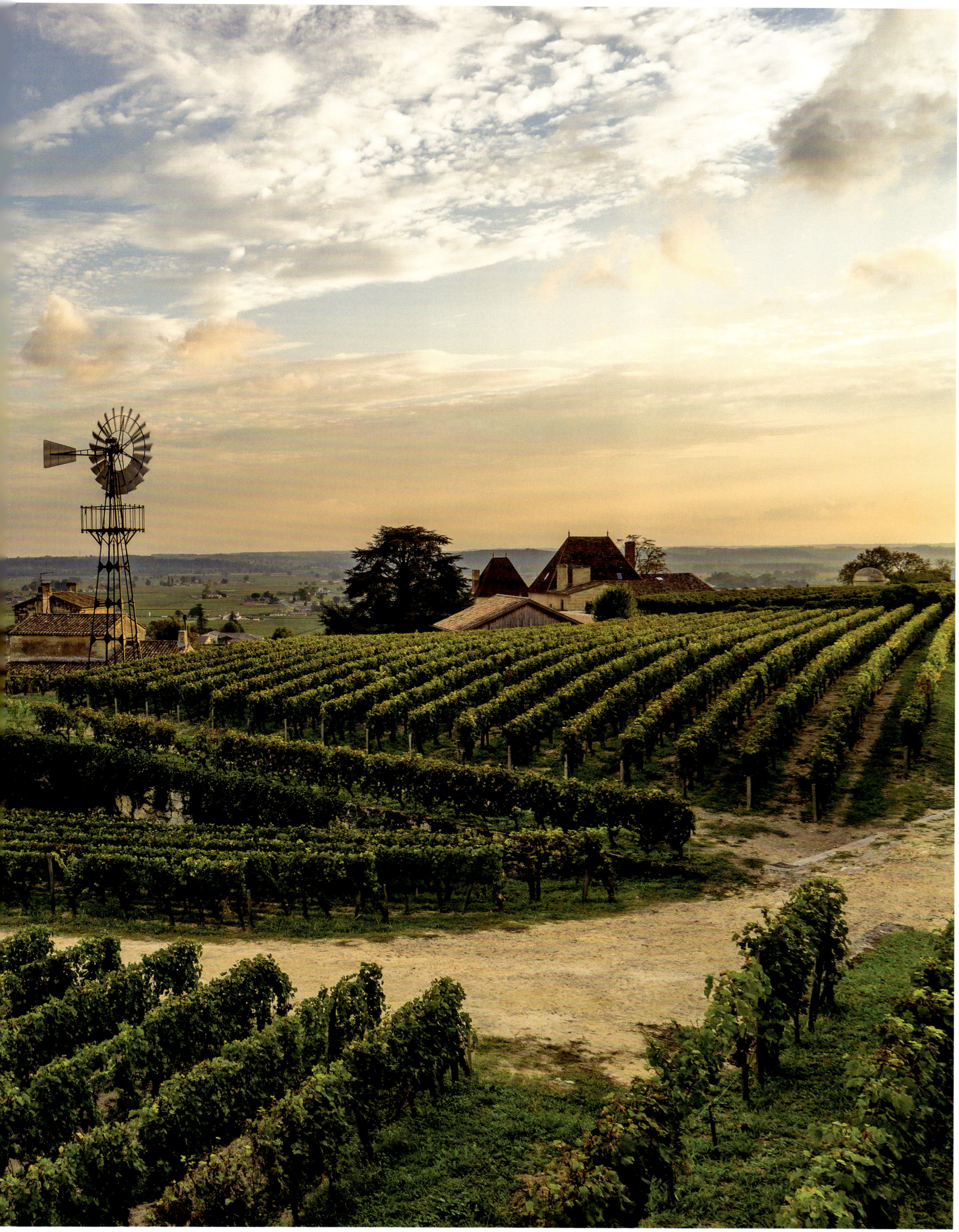

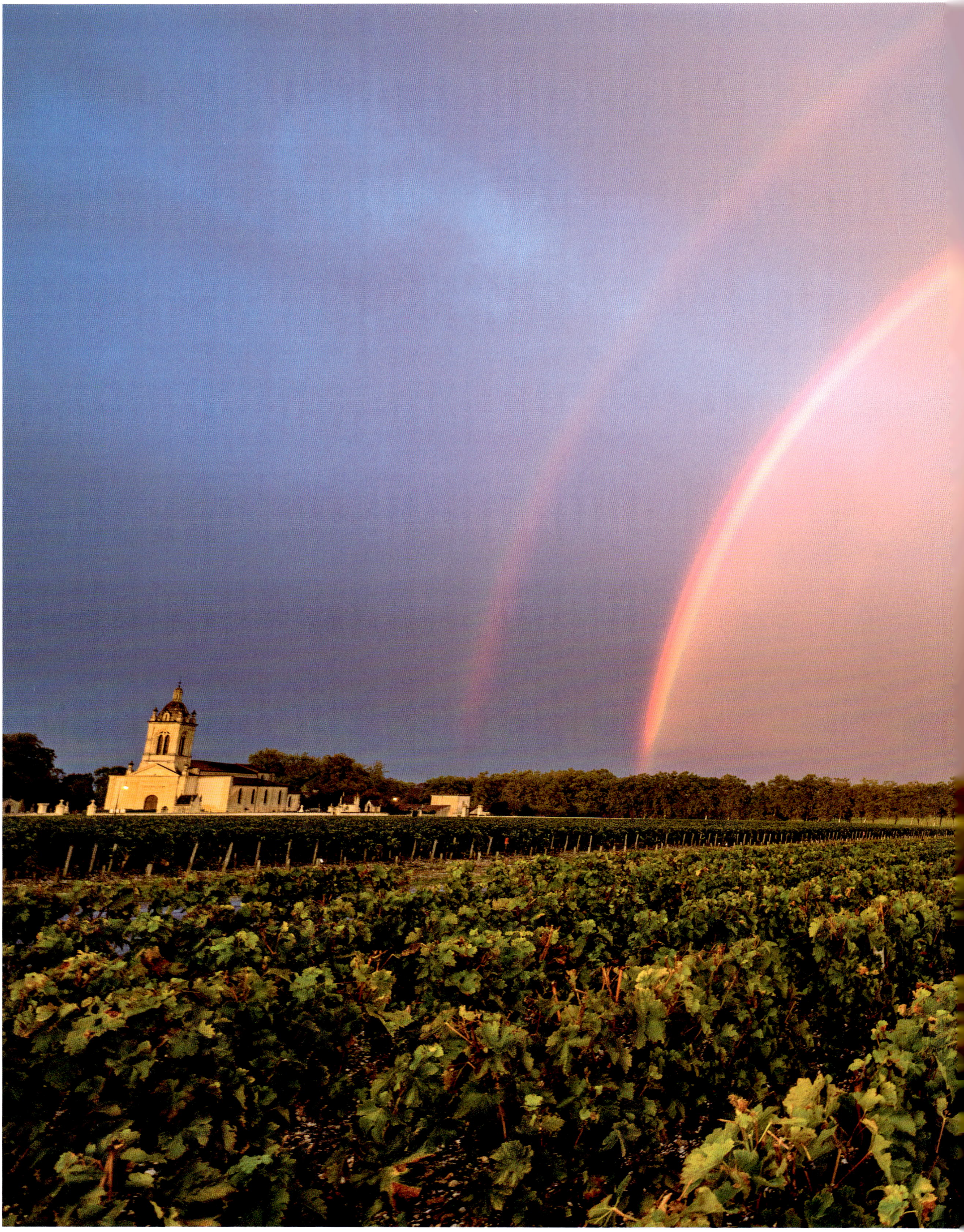

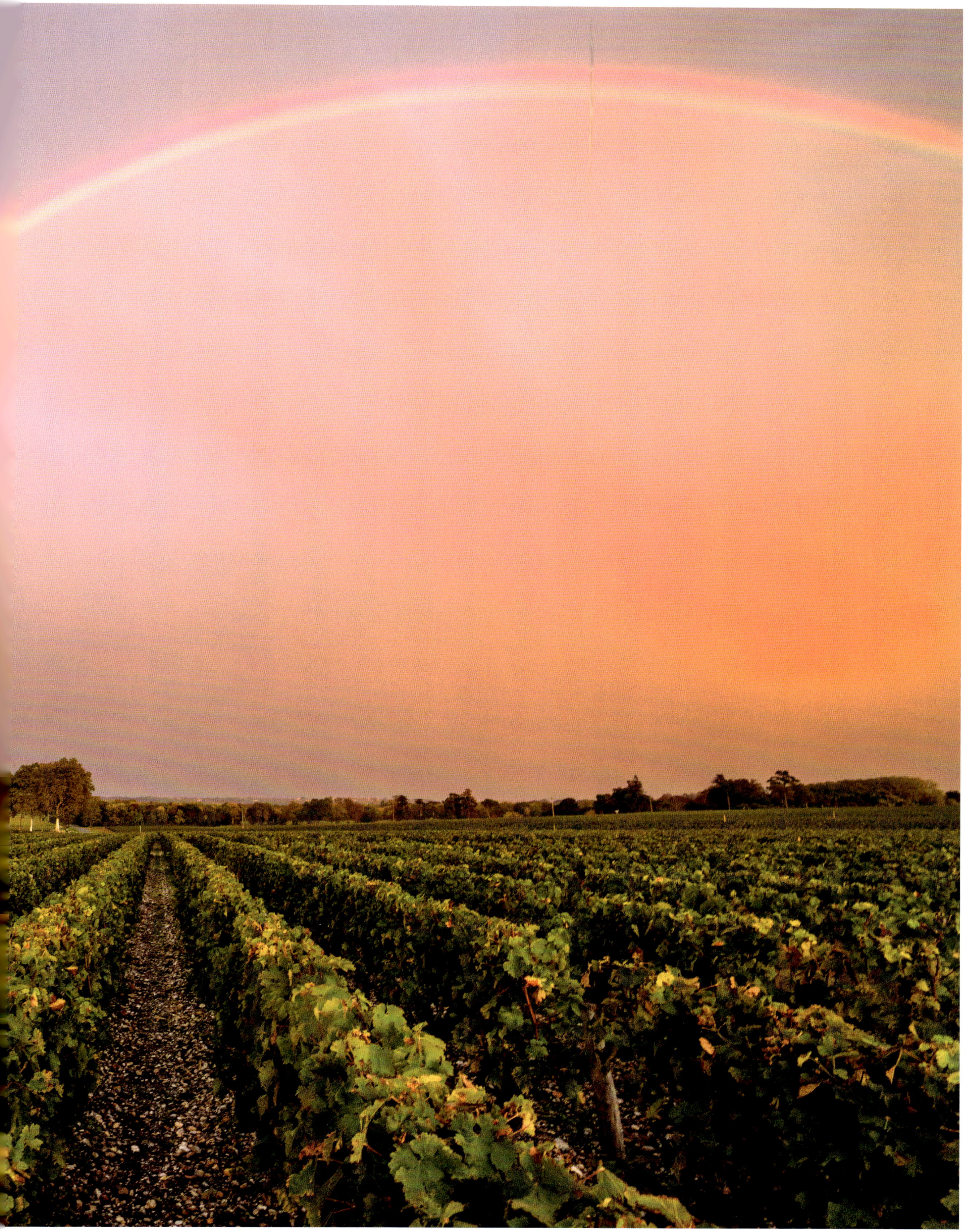

Petrus

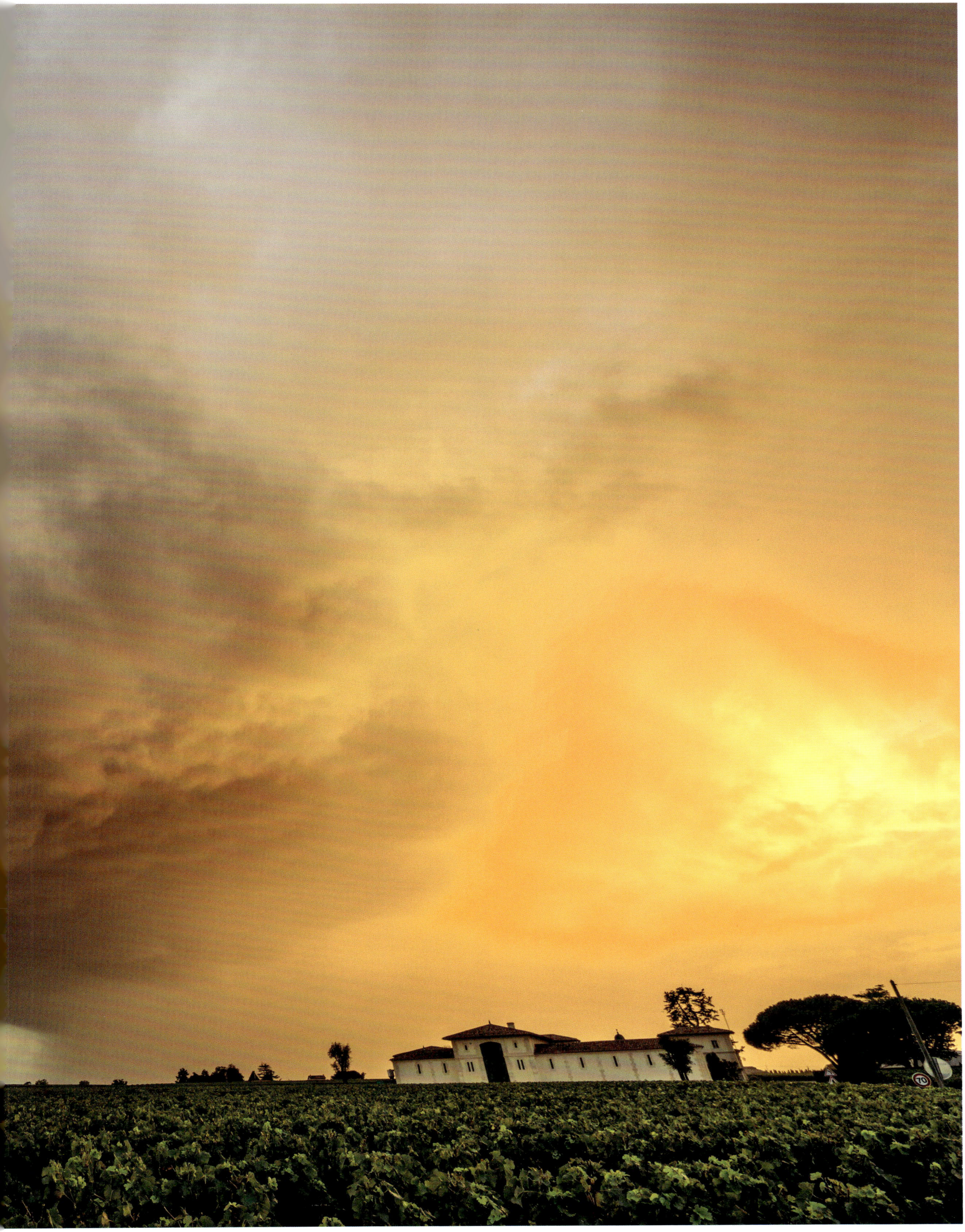

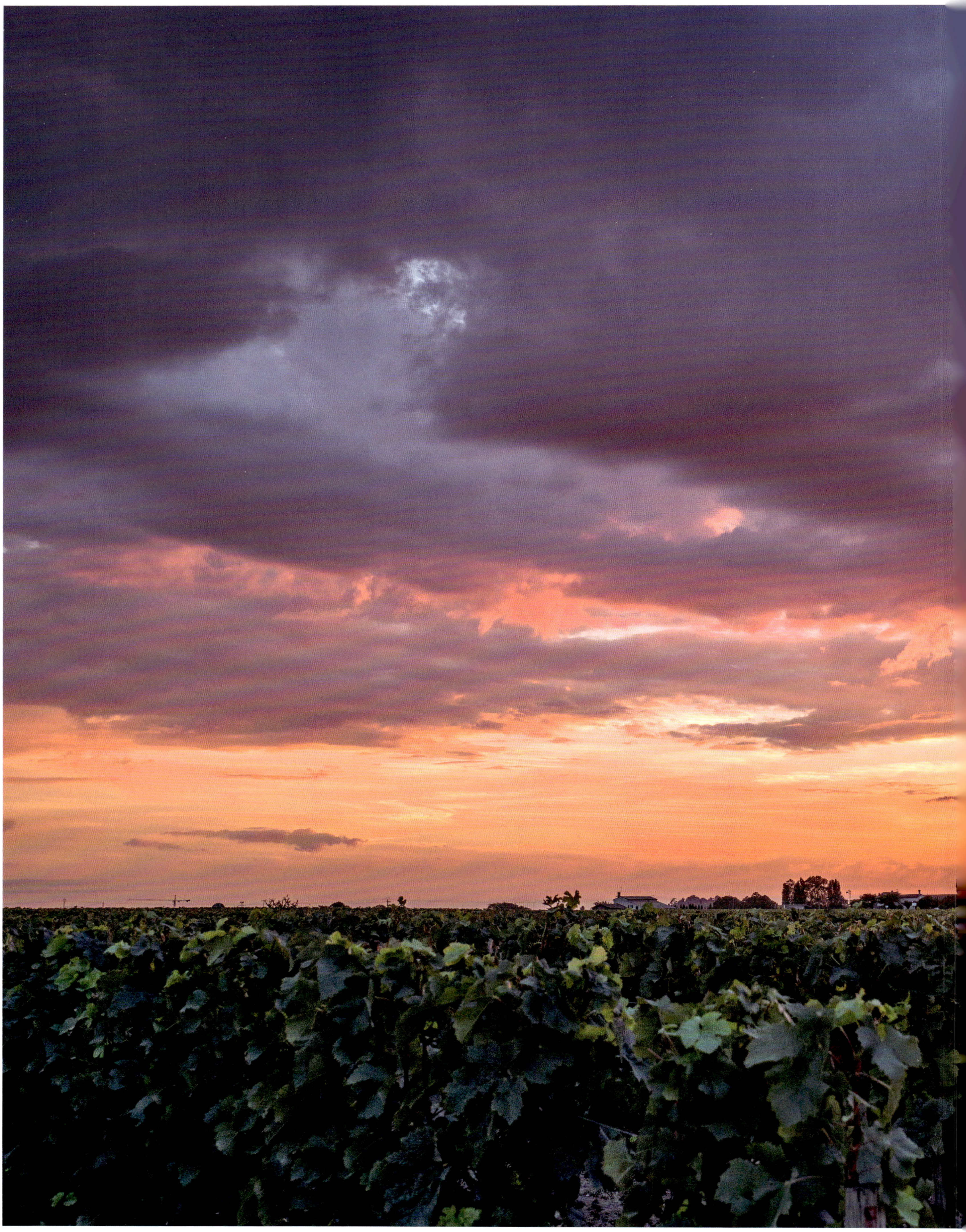

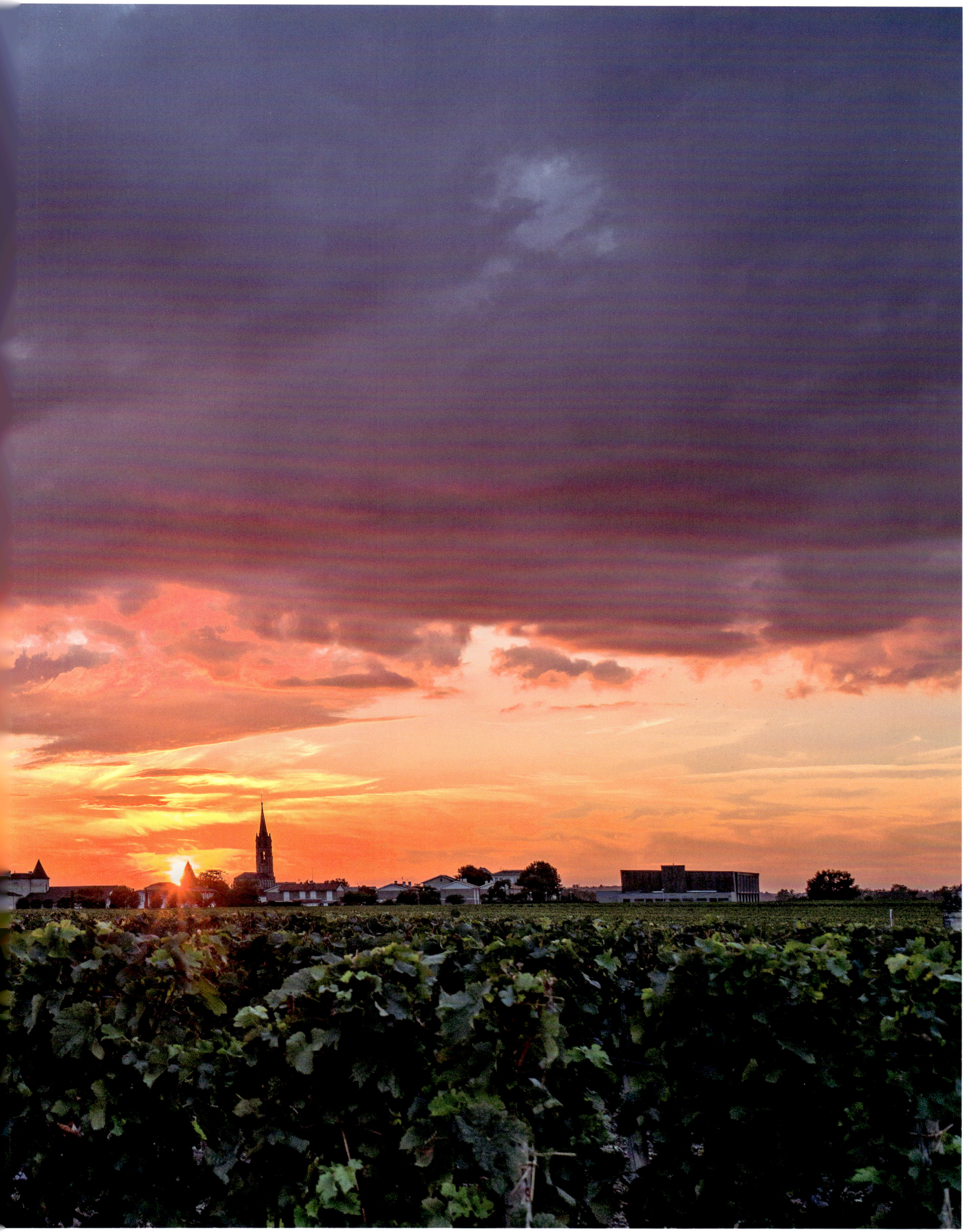

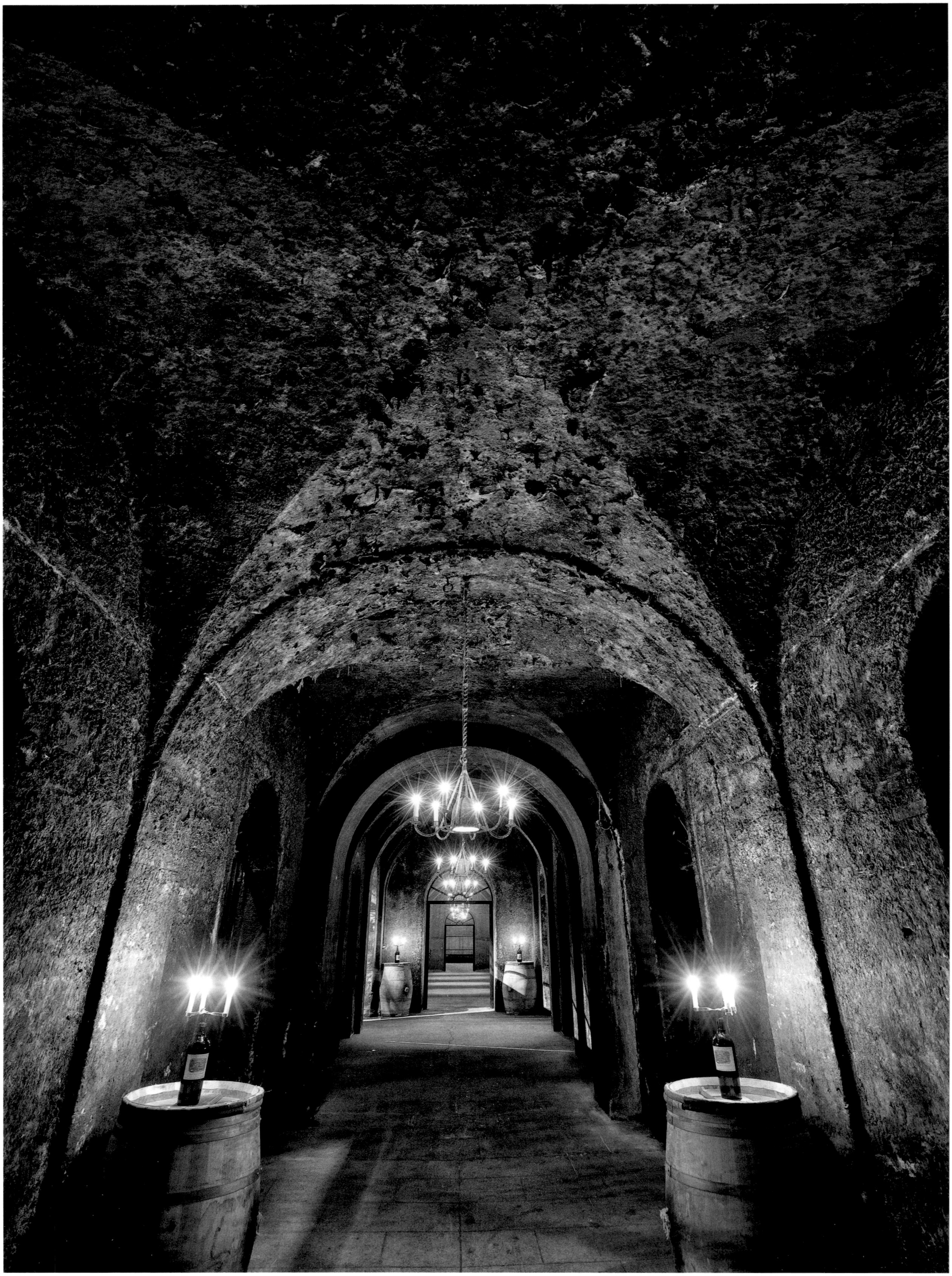

CHÂTEAU LAFITE ROTHSCHILD 1855
FIRST GROWTH, AOC PAUILLAC

You don't get to be Lafite Rothschild if history weighs you down.

This is a place that was already making waves in 1150, when legend has it that a certain Eleanor of Aquitaine spent a few nights in the Seigneurie de La Hite, just two years before she married Henri Plantagenet of England and brought the wine lands of Bordeaux as her wedding gift. Even then, La Hite – meaning high ground in the local dialect – was a vast domain that extended close to 2,500 acres to the north of Pauillac, bordered by the Garonne river to one side and heading through the Breuil marshes over to the village of Milon and the plateau of Carruades. Local records reveal livestock rearing was taking place on farmland in La Hite less than 80 years later.

And as befits these ancient origins, the Lafite Rothschild that you arrive at today, on that same raised hillock to the northern reaches of Pauillac, is the oldest château building of the Club of Nine, dating back a full 200 years prior to the French Revolution, to 1572. It has been modernised since, of course: first through lavish refurbishments by Baroness Betty de Rothschild in the 1870s, then painstaking restoration by Baroness Liliane after the ravages of World War Two.

Head into these drawing rooms, with their fabric-covered walls in rich shades of red, blue and yellow, and you can feel the stirrings of history alongside the Baroness' famous flair for interior design and love of silks, damasks, velvets and brocades. Or better yet, head down to the château's wine library and cellar, in a vaulted stone room that is accessed via a false cupboard door installed to protect its contents from discovery when enemy soldiers were billeted in the château. Follow the worn flagstone steps and you find dusty rows of bottles in boxes labelled 1797, 1798, 1799… right through the centuries to the early 1900s. It's clear that long-ago ghosts protect this precious nectar.

And there are few more precious wines than Lafite Rothschild. Even when the Rothschilds first became owners, successfully bidding at auction back in 1868, they recovered the purchase price within a decade due to the profitability of the wine.

Legendary for its ability to develop over time, Lafite is the result of a process that has been perfected over centuries. Right from its earliest years the winemakers of Bordeaux have been known for their skill at blending – the careful bedding together of different grapes and soil types.

So how do you blend Château Lafite Rothschild, one of the most eagerly awaited and beloved wines in the world? Not an easy question, still less an easy task.

The man to ask is Eric Kohler, technical director of the Domaines Barons de Rothschild Bordeaux estates. He talks through the process with the skill and precision of a grand master. For the first few months after harvest, the barrels of cabernet sauvignon, merlot, cabernet franc and petit verdot will be kept separate, gaining form and character until the meticulous process of blending gets underway.

First, Kohler says, there is the visual side. 'Lafite doesn't have to be as inky as some wines, but as a Pauillac it does require a certain visual strength and richness,' he says. 'If the colour is not strong it may provoke questions about the ripeness of the fruit, because the cabernet sauvignon that dominates the blend is a fairly small grape with a thick, deeply coloured skin that when ripe will easily share that colour with its juice. If the colour of any one barrel is not particularly strong but the nose and palate still fragrant, it may provide a perfect contribution to the blend, but not the heart.

'On the nose,' he continues, 'we are looking for fruit that gives the character of the year, and its best aromatic expression. Some vintages see grapes ripen under large amounts of sunshine and have a ripe almost cooked fruit character, while others have fresh fruit and still others slightly lean, just-ripe aromatics. We must respect that and give expression to the essential character of a vintage, but we are also looking for a sense of complexity. For Lafite we need a spectrum of flavours rather than a strong expression of any particular one – our strength lies in an ensemble of impressions, from dark autumnal fruits to fragrant plants and herbs, and all with a sense of freshness and elegance.

'On the palate, a great Lafite is rich but not impenetrable. It must have concentration but not simply for its own sake. The type and style of tannins found in the skins and pips of the grape are key – concentrated tannins are easy to extract, while fine and supple ones are more difficult but more sought after.'

The subtle balance between all of these elements and the difficulty of drawing out their best expression is where the greatness of the terroir at Château Lafite Rothschild becomes clear. Certain plots of these astonishing soils give more colour to the grapes, others more aromatic expression, others a certain austerity, others richness and concentration.

Kohler and his colleagues can choose from a rich palette of flavours, textures and structures, adhering to the essential truth that blending means thinking not only about the wine's expression today, but how it will lead to a bottle that can sit quietly in the cellars, gathering strength, conviction and beauty over the many years ahead. And how each bottle will stand as a testament upon opening to the meticulous decisions taken by an entire team from bud burst to harvest, from blending to ageing, as they look to do justice to the infinite potential of this land.

Size and production 276 acres, makes an average of 18,000 cases per year across Lafite Rothschild and Carruades de Lafite.
Owner Baron Eric de Rothschild (Fourth generation since Baron James de Rothschild purchased the estate in 1868).

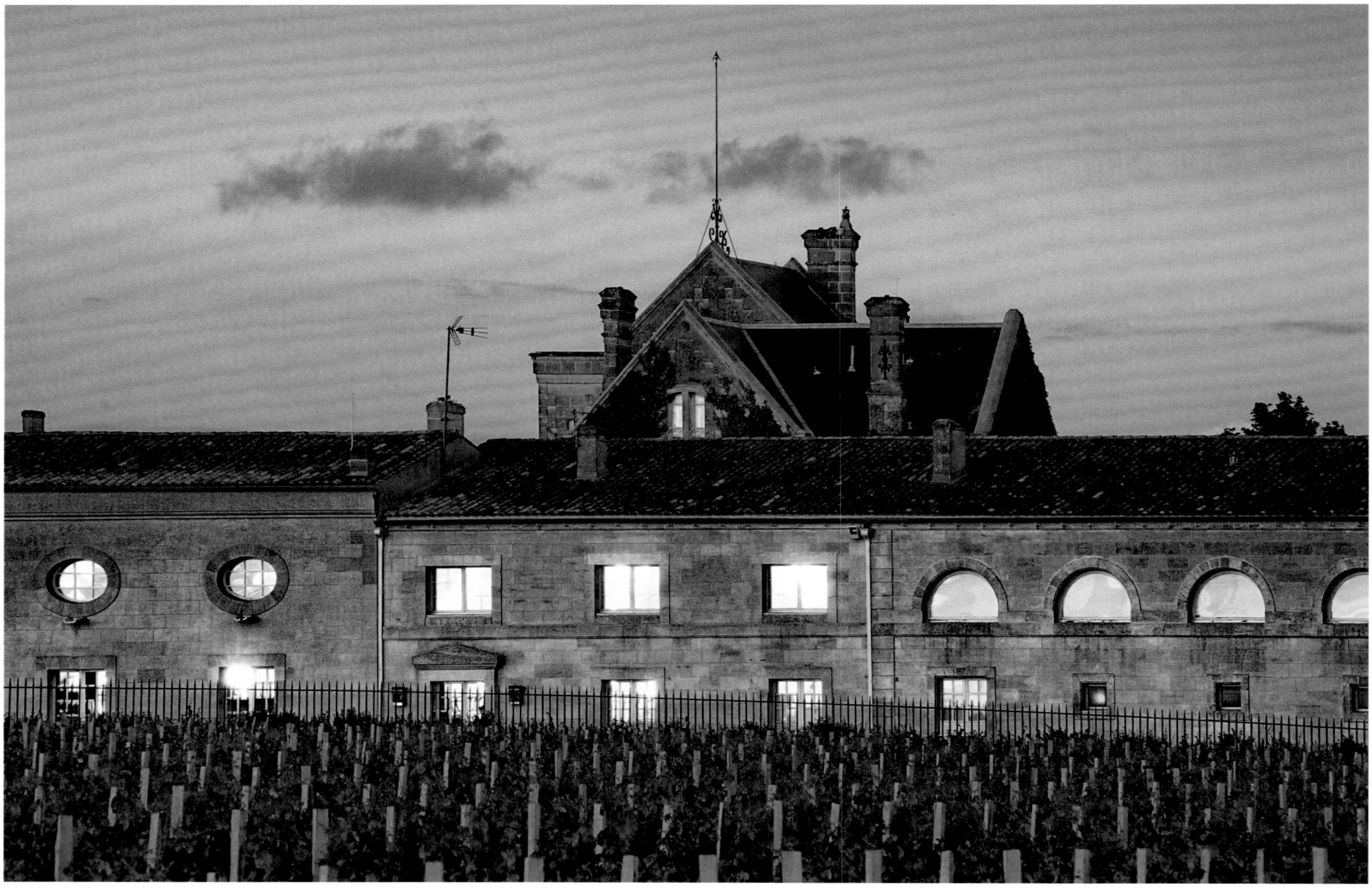

CHÂTEAU MOUTON ROTHSCHILD
1855 FIRST GROWTH AOC PAUILLAC

The gravel stretches in all directions here, a ripple of greys and charcoals. Tiny slivers of slate sit next to plump pudding stones and glistening quartz drawn from the Massif Central and the Pyrenees mountains, brought here during the last known glacial period in Europe 2 million years ago. There is not just a horizontal spread through this vineyard but vertical also, heading down six metres beneath our feet.

It took a little longer for the soils to be revealed in this part of Bordeaux than it did elsewhere. The waters did not fully recede from this spot until Dutch experts were called upon to put their engineering skills to use building ditches and drainage channels in the first half of the 17th century.

To understand why, you simply have to look around. Pauillac sits halfway up the Médoc peninsula, stranded between the Garonne river to the east – its grey waters are just within sight from up here on the Grand Plateau, the highest point of the Mouton vineyard at 40 metres above sea level – and the Atlantic Ocean to the west.

Today home to the greatest cabernet sauvignon-based wines in the world, the area was under water, or remained at best damp marshland with intermittent farms, until local landowners were given sufficient incentives to employ those Dutch engineers.

This particular piece of land plays a crucial role in the history of how that happened. The first steps were taken in 1627 when the Royal French forces were fighting the Huguenots in La Rochelle, a little further up the Atlantic coast. Leading the troops was the owner of Mouton, Jean-Louis de Nogaret de la Valette, the Duc d'Eperon, a military commander who was awarded the title Admiral of France.

Valette played a key role in the blockade of La Rochelle by both sea and land, but it turns out that his more lasting achievement came from meeting a Dutch hydraulic engineer during the siege called Jan Adriaasz Leeghwater. At some point between battling Huguenots, Valette asked Leeghwater to draw up a plan for draining the marshes of the Médoc, and on his return to Bordeaux found the local parliament more than willing to support the project.

Leeghwater came up with an ambitious drainage scheme that allowed previously unused land to be reclaimed, and revealed a series of gravelly outcrops across the peninsula where today such complex, nuanced wines begin their life. And it was the gravel – specifically its ability to store heat and reflect it back to the grapes, and to drain away the water from those Atlantic Ocean rains – that would prove so perfectly adapted to cabernet sauvignon, the key component of the great wines of Left Bank Bordeaux.

But we're not done with Mouton's role in the growth of cabernet sauvignon quite yet. Fast forward 150 years, to when Baron Hector de Brane becomes owner of Mouton and sets about building up the size of its vineyard. In the years following the French Revolution through to the mid-1700s, he established himself as a visionary of the vineyards, encouraging the widespread planting of cabernet sauvignon as the grape most suited to the soils of Pauillac.

At this time, cabernet sauvignon was just making its first appearance in the world's vineyards, the result of a natural cross between two older grapes of Bordeaux – sauvignon blanc and cabernet franc – that had been growing next to each other for centuries in vineyards that had little formal planting schemes.

Did the heat of the Médoc soils provoke this cross-pollination? We don't know exactly where the first cabernet sauvignon plants were born, but we do know that Baron Hector, then his son Jacques-Maxime, and later the Rothschilds' vineyard director Théodore Galos, all championed the use of this grape variety. For many of the later years of the 19th century, the château is recorded as using solely cabernet sauvignon in its wines.

We also know that the Grand Plateau of Mouton – the same plateau becomes that of Lafite as the neighbouring vines glide into one another – is perfectly suited to nurture this richly scented, thick-skinned yet capricious grape, that chooses only to release its blackcurrant, liquorice and wild mint aromatics when fully ripe. And the dense composition of the soils here, with an astonishingly profound 98% gravel and just 2% clay, means that cabernet sauvignon reaches that optimum ripeness year after year.

It is why this plateau is home to the oldest vines of Château Mouton Rothschild. Found in the plot named La Baronne Philippine, they are close to 120 years old. The entire plot covers two and a half acres of land, and rows 195 to 333 and 338 to 350 have not been replanted since 1900. They are joined by equally old vines in plots named Baronne Pauline, Grand Plantey and Raoul. In total Mouton has a full 13 acres of these gnarled old characters – practically unheard of in Bordeaux.

Yet you might not know it to look at them. The vines grow very slowly here precisely because of the poor quality of the soils, so plants that are into their second century are still barely wider than an upper arm. Instead, they conserve their energy for their fruit. The fact that they have survived so long tells you just how well they have done their job. It also reminds us of how this pile of stones helped cabernet sauvignon, a grape that has since spread around the world and been responsible for many of the most celebrated and iconic wines of all time, get its first shot of publicity back in 18th-century Bordeaux.

Size and production 207 acres, makes an average of 12,000 cases per year across Mouton Rothschild, Le Petit Mouton and white wine Aile d'Argent.
Owners Philippe Sereys de Rothschild, Camille Sereys de Rothschild, Julien de Beaumarchais de Rothschild (Fifth generation since Baron Nathaniel de Rothschild purchased the estate in 1853).
Promoted to First Growth in 1973 (named Second Growth in 1855)

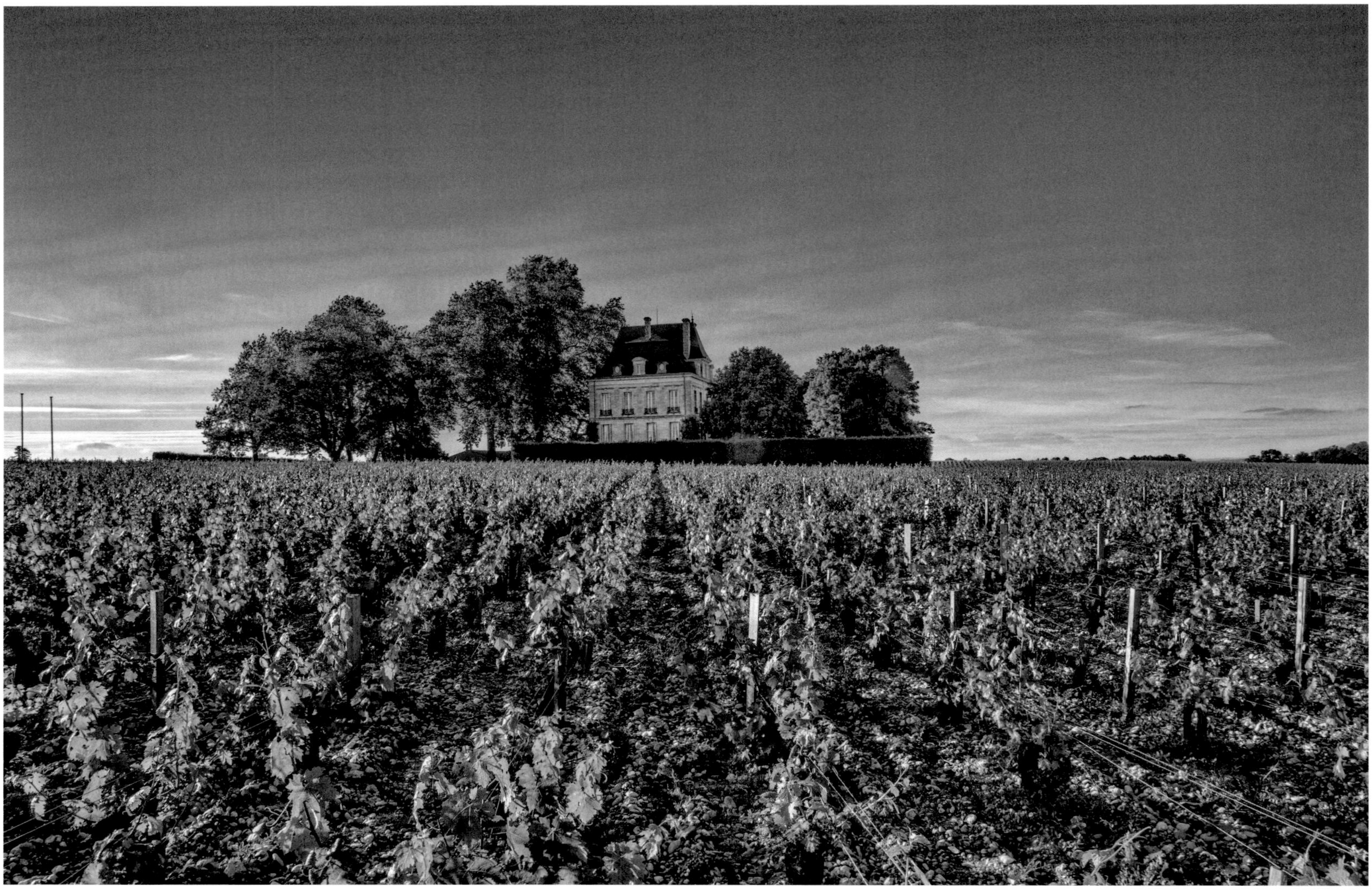

CHÂTEAU LATOUR 1855
FIRST GROWTH, AOC PAUILLAC

To have three First Growths in Pauillac seems a little greedy, but there they are, staking the appellation's claim to be the single greatest stretch of soil in Bordeaux. Latour is the final figure of the triumvirate, and is the most southerly of the three, grazing the border with Saint Julien. Like all of the Médoc Firsts, the Garonne is within easy walking distance of the château, although once the vines finish there is a good 70 acres of meadow before you reach its banks. Today you'll find cows grazing on this land, but soon they'll be replaced by the nine Percheron, Breton and Ardenne horses that have been used to work the vines of Latour since 2008.

If ever you need to remember that these blockbuster, dizzyingly priced wines are also part of a long agrarian tradition, take a stroll down to this meadow. Standing at this point, looking back up towards the château with the curves of its dovecote (or less poetically its 17th-century pigeon house) rising from the vines, the sense of proportion flows over you. This is not the original tower that gave Latour its name but a replacement of the fortified guard post built in the 1330s by the Gaucelme de Castillon to defend against French insurgents, and yet it still provides an anchor to the gentle swell of vines.

All around, the vineyard's hollows and crests rise and fall with the heartbeat of the land. This is L'Enclos de Latour – the 116-acre walled vineyard that forms the heart of the estate. There is a variety of soil types within the low-lying stone walls, with some sections thick with the same famous Pauillac gravels you find at Mouton and Lafite, and others rich in a form of sticky clay more typically found at Petrus that perfectly moderates the flow of water to the vines and gives Latour a distinctive character all of its own, by turns powerful and structured yet densely fragranced and soaringly fresh.

A large rose garden, home to more than two dozen varieties, flourishes to one side, while newly planted hedgerows encourage ever-greater forms of biodiversity. Three specially designed containers for stirring – or dynamising – the biodynamic treatments that govern viticulture here are kept under a lean-to shelter, ready to prepare the flowers and plant tinctures that will be applied to the grapes at different stages of the growing cycle. At the end of the rows of vines, tiny white and pink blooms push alongside the roses, most notably the tiny white chamomile flowers that are used for the tinctures and have started to grow wild as a result.

There are few places in Bordeaux that offer such a clear example of the practical meaning of terroir. Everything at Latour demands that you slow down, take your time, get close to what is really happening in each corner of these vines and learn to read the specificities of the land. The technical team at this First Growth château believes that this is the real beauty of using biodynamic and organic treatments. Both philosophies form just part of the precision agriculture of this estate, and are underpinned by a ranger of technologies, from satellite images and sensors assessing vine vigour to the regular use of surf websites to check the swell and wind direction before applying any treatments. For the past five years, they have been studying 40 of the estate's 138 plots both inside and outside of L'Enclos to form an accurate map of the vines' reactions to challenges through the growing season.

But the idea is not to 'drown in analysis', as technical director Hélène Genin puts it. Rather it is to use it to underline and explain traditional approaches. It is only by applying natural vineyard treatments by hand and closely following individual rows of vines that you can truly understand how different plots will react. It builds on the slow work of centuries of men and women who brought the best out of these soils, and allows for a clearer overall picture of the Latour vineyard than a conventional approach of tractors and machines can ever permit.

Even the use of horses reflects this. The most able horses are male, usually aged between two and seven years old. They sometimes find it tough to work heavy clays after rainfall, and yet they force a change of pace, ensuring you slow down and become aware of what is happening around you. They lessen the risk of cutting corners.

The Club of Nine estates owe everything to the careful stewardship of former generations. These forms of viticulture are a sign of respect to that history, to the health of the men and women working in the vineyards today, and a way to farm sustainably that can be handed down to future generations. Essentially Latour is putting more in to the land than it is taking out – and at the same time showing a healthy dose of understanding that wine lovers pay handsomely for the price of entry to this club, and in return are looking for an unadulterated taste of the land.

'Simply having the terroir is already a gift,' says Genin. 'But it means nothing if you don't learn how to interpret and protect it, and nurture its potential.'

Size and production 230 acres, makes an average of 25,000 cases per year across Latour, Les Forts de Latour and Pauillac (de Latour).
Owner Artémis Domaines (Pinault family) since 1993.

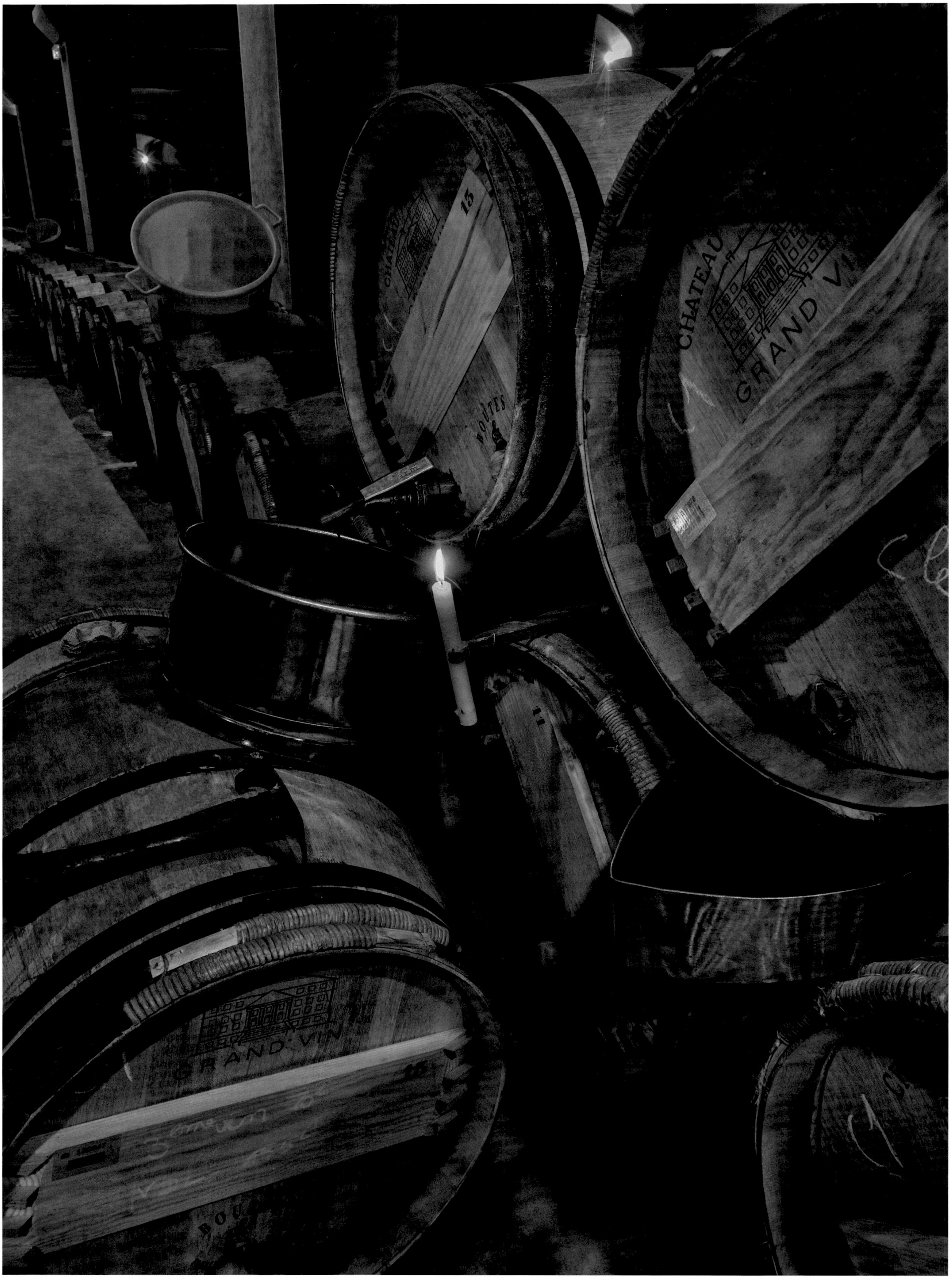
CHATEAU
GRAND VIN
GRAND VIN

CHÂTEAU MARGAUX 1855
FIRST GROWTH AOC MARGAUX

The perfume of Château Margaux is just one way in which this estate, perhaps more than any other member of the Club of Nine, refuses to play by the rules. A Left Bank First Growth – which means a production level of somewhere upwards of 100,000 bottles and endless rows of vines under its stewardship – with the grace, elegance and supple movement of a Musigny grand cru. A cabernet sauvignon-dominated wine with the most sublimely delicate and yet powerfully heady perfume – a rose garden after a summer downpour – one that can make you laugh in sheer surprise at how such aromatic complexity can curl upwards from a glass.

But this is the essence of Château Margaux: a lesson in the power of great wine to surprise us, move us, provoke us. Its success comes from a mosaic of tiny details, laid next to each other, beside each other, atop each other, that add up to something extraordinary. Every inch of this land is conceived in beauty, from the 45 acres of vines that grow within the stone walls of this château's very own Enclos to the vein of gravel that widens out to the legendary Puch Sem Peyre plot, where the heart of the estate's best vines are grown. This plot has been recognised as growing exceptional quality grapes for over 500 years, conferring density and richness to the wine, and breadth to the aromatics. Not that you'd know it to look at the near-impenetrable gravels in this plot, but countless archival documents stored in the graceful drawing rooms overlooking the park speak of the power of Puch Sem Peyre, and how its name refers to a 'puch' or well because the soils are so gravelly that you can dig a well from them with your bare hands.

Château Margaux is also the only one of the Club of Nine that has no sister properties elsewhere – no wine merchant business, no second projects to draw the gaze away.

'I never wanted to focus on other things,' owner Corinne Mentzelopoulos says. 'There is always so much to do at Margaux, and every time we make one small change it leads to so many others. I consider each time, what does this bring to Margaux? What does it add? Do I even have the right?'

Mentzelopoulos instinctively recognises the role that individual families have played in building up all of these properties, one passing down to the next over the centuries – in this case from the Lords of La Mothe de Margaux in the 1400s through to the Lestonnac family of Bordeaux parliamentarians who guided its growth from the 1500s right through to the late 1700s, allowing for two centuries of stable and continual excellence. In more recent years, the Greek origins of the Mentzelopoulos family – that arrived with André Mentzelopoulos in 1977 – symbolise the vast and varied history of Bordeaux. They show how its greatest wines have been embraced by cultures around the world since time immemorial, and its system of production and commerce built by successive waves of international wine lovers and merchants.

While we know that great wines come from the multitude of events happening far below ground, let's not pretend that terroir does not need a steady and inspired pair of hands to free its voice. And the inevitability of this particular family arriving here is striking. The château building of Margaux has been a symbol of grace and beauty since it was first unveiled in 1815, summed up in its Palladian-style neo-classical columns that stand along its façade, inspired by the Parthenon in Athens. The original architect, Louis Combes, explained that he was passionate about this style of architecture because of its 'unity, simplicity, balance... [it] is driven by necessity, guided by reason, pared back by taste and genius.'

'The symbolism of this architecture and its nod to the roots of civilisation in Classical Greece is something of huge importance to me,' Mentzelopoulos says. 'The fact that it represents the bringing together of different cultures moves me deeply. It is a symbol of the power of wine to connect cultures, to bridge different peoples, nationalities, ages and political persuasions. The nuances and complexities in wine are a reflection of our own differences.'

'Château Margaux is a place of great peace, calm and quiet to reflect upon this,' she continues. 'It is a place where you are constantly aware of the privilege that being an owner here affords, and the debt that we owe in return. There is a duty that comes with being the custodian of this land. It is why we must question ourselves constantly, each time that we make a change to the wine, to the buildings, to the gardens, even to the pathway leading up to the château. To do something without thinking deeply on its consequences is impossible.'

Attention to detail, Château Margaux tells us, is essential in the creation of great wine. But doubt plays an equal part.

Size and production 244 acres, makes an average of 11,000 cases per year across Margaux, Pavillon Rouge and white wine Pavillon Blanc.
Owner Corinne Mentzelopoulos (Second generation since André Mentzelopoulos bought the estate in 1977).

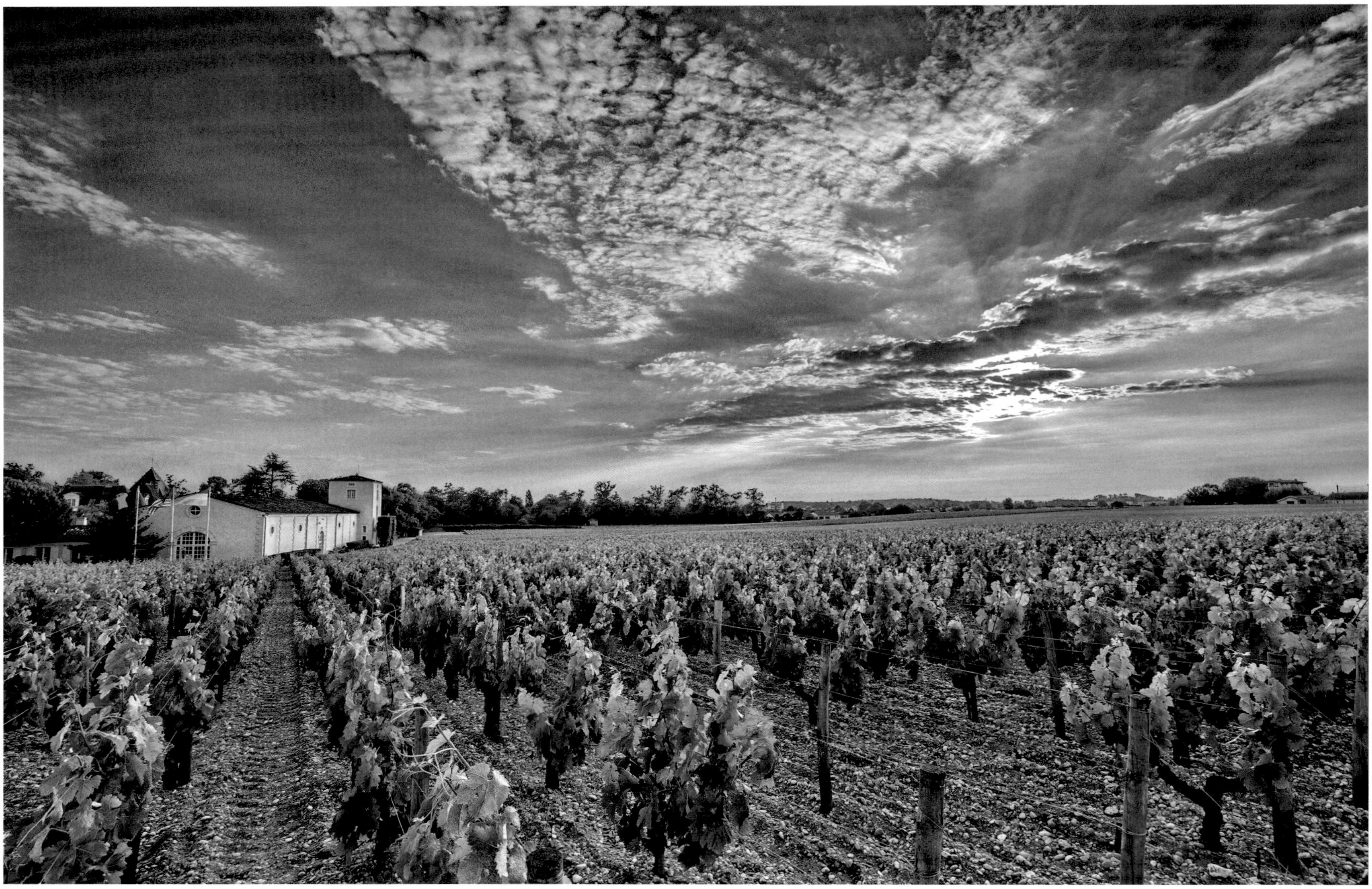

CHÂTEAU HAUT-BRION 1855
FIRST GROWTH AOC PESSAC LÉOGNAN

Château Haut-Brion stands alone for several reasons. Firstly, in its geography, as it is the only 1855 First Growth wine that lies outside of the Médoc peninsula in the appellation of Pessac Léognan, which sits close to the city of Bordeaux. And it is also the only one of the Club of Nine to be recognised in two classifications: both 1855 and the 1953 ranking of the best estates of the historic Graves appellation.

This place has a fair claim to be named the birthplace of fine wine. And we can pinpoint not only when but where and why this is the case if we head to the group of low-lying buildings set out around a cobbled courtyard known as the Cour des Artisans. For many centuries, vines grew on this spot, but today it is the heart of Haut-Brion, named in honour of the workshops used by ironmongers, blacksmiths, gardeners and carpenters that were historically needed to maintain the smooth running of the château.

Until the Middle Ages, one essential element of wine production would still have been made in downtown Bordeaux and brought here only on completion – the barrels that provided a vessel for first making the wine and then for transporting it to merchants and clients once finished. A variety of wood was typically used for barrels, from oak to chestnut to fir to acacia. Although they were the best available product for both tasks, they would frequently break apart, their staves split or dislodged, particularly when being transported by cart over stony ground. Once split, their contents risked being lost, or the contact with the outside air risked turning the wine inside to vinegar. Barrels were, in short, an imperfect vessel.

We don't know exactly when Haut-Brion's Arnaud III de Pontac began experimenting with ways to improve them but we do know that in this estate, some time close to 400 years ago, experiments with a new style of barrel began that would lead to the birth of the New French Claret that signalled the definitive move towards the fine wine style of today. And we have an exact date when the wider world sat up and took notice: Friday 10 April 1663, when Samuel Pepys wrote in his diary about a new French claret called Ho Bryan with 'a good and most particular taste that I never met with'.

How did this happen? The 17th century was the age of empiricism, when ideas were being tested, proven and advanced through practical experimentation. We know that Pontac was an exceptionally well-read man, with one of the greatest libraries in Europe. He was also a politician in the Bordeaux parliament and a committed vintner who was very likely to have had the early books on viticulture that were now appearing. His brilliance seems to have been in taking the various cutting-edge ideas of the time and bringing them together in his own workshops. His tests included the use of oak as the wood of choice; iron hoops wrapped around the outside of the barrel to strengthen its resistance; the use of the Dutch sulphur candle to disinfect the inside and protect the wine against spoilage; the clearing out of the lees cells during ageing to provide a natural clarification; the topping up of barrels with extra wine to prevent oxidation; keeping the grape skins in contact with the juice for long enough to fully extract their colour, aromatics and tannin. Haut-Brion became a centre of experimentation, and through this defined a new style of winemaking.

'The stabilisation of wine that came through mastering barrel ageing was key to unlocking the potential of the soil, and of wine itself,' says Jean-Philippe Masclef, technical director of Haut-Brion. 'As so often in wine, our ancestors found the right way to do things and then later science proved that they were right.'

It was the moment that everything changed in the production of the world's great wines – and yet head to the flagstone-floored barrel workshop today and time seems to have stood still. The sweet smell of oak hangs in the air as cooper Luc Nicolas assembles each individual barrel by hand, carefully selecting and weighing up the 27 individual staves that make up each one, then coaxing the iron hoop over the outside and holding the barrel over an open fire to gently char its inside and render the oak soft enough to be hammered into its final position.

The basic form and technique has not changed for centuries. Instead the biggest developments in recent years centre around research into the types of oak; its origin not just in terms of different forests around France but individual locations and plots within those forests. There is a growing understanding of the impact this makes on aromatic and gustatory compounds that impart extra layers of flavour and complexity to a nascent wine. Three of the Club of Nine – Haut-Brion, Lafite and Margaux – maintain their own cooperage, illuminating and strengthening the unshakeable bond between grape and oak.

Size and production 127 acres, makes an average of 7,000 cases per year across Haut-Brion, Le Clarence de Haut-Brion and white wine Haut-Brion Blanc.
Owner Prince Robert of Luxembourg (Third generation since great-grandfather Clarence Dillon bought the estate in 1935).

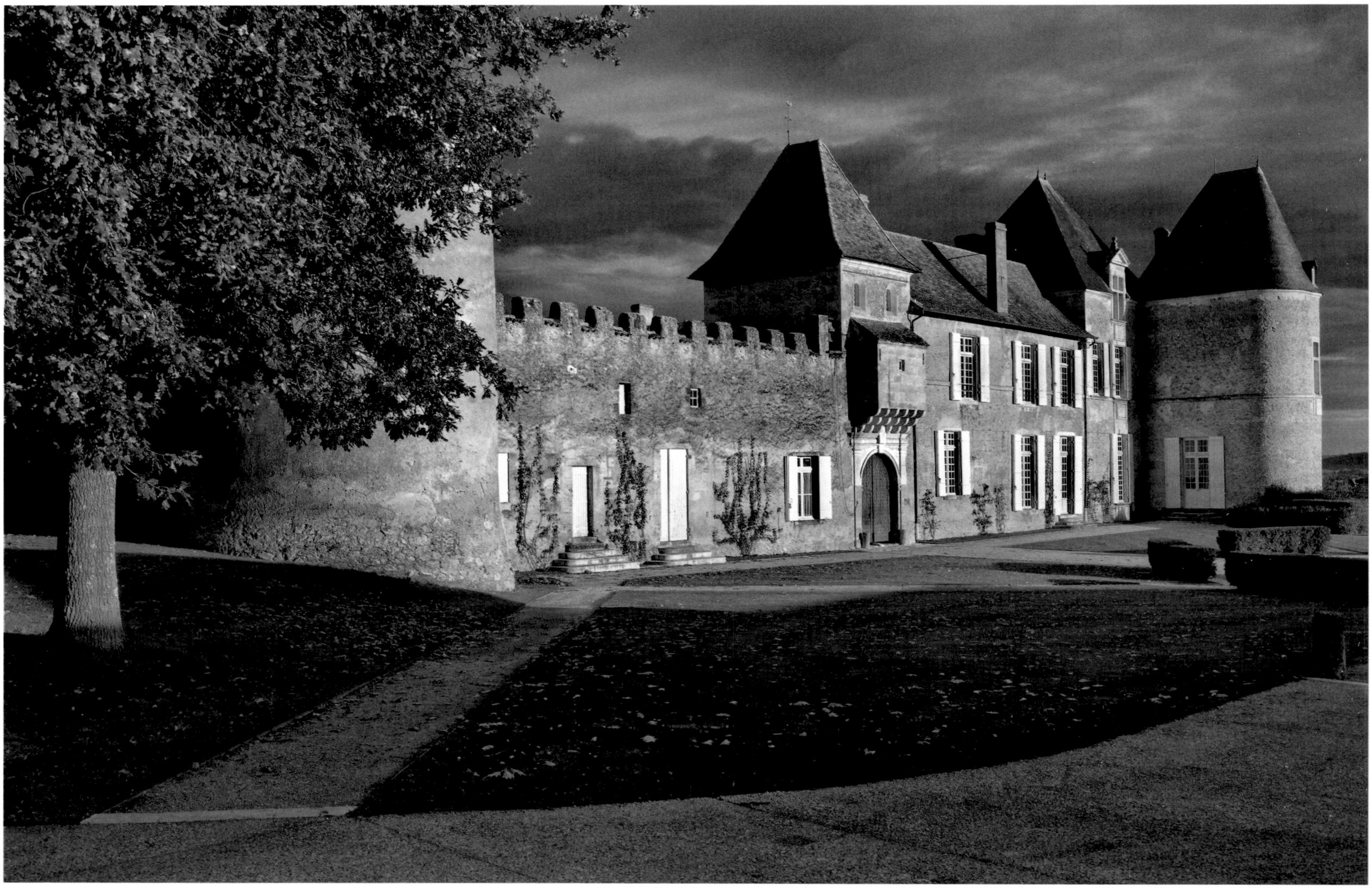

CHÂTEAU YQUEM 1855
FIRST GROWTH SUPERIOR AOC SAUTERNES

We need to start a different conversation altogether when it comes to Yquem.

Designated in 1855 as the First Growth to end all First Growths – *Premier Cru Supérieur* – reportedly not only because of its wines selling to Tsars and royalty all over Europe but also because the 1847 vintage blew everyone out of the water and they were still talking about it seven (okay 170) years later. If you want to find an 1855 vintage that will still taste stunning, this is the place to come.

Despite this, Yquem is today the symbol of a style of wine that is – how shall we put this – niche, artisan, increasingly rare. Little by little we are forgetting how to consume these wines, and one of the great challenges is finding consumers willing to appreciate a sweet style that can contain somewhere between 120 and 150 grams of residual sugar, and yet can feel as light as a feather inching across a satin skirt.

This challenge is just part of why Yquem is the true face of humility. The most stunning property, the most exquisite taste, and yet a reminder of our fragility. You simply cannot pretend that anything other than nature rules here.

For a start, its very existence is dependent on the most capricious and narrow of parameters. There are few spots on earth that can produce the conditions needed for a wine like Yquem. If you want to understand the true link between soils, climate, grape variety and wine style – the heart of the often-disputed notion of terroir – here it is.

Sauternes is a land shaped by water, set to the south of the Garonne Valley and north of the Landes plateau on a succession of small hills and outcrops. Its climate is influenced by the ever-present Garonne river that defines all of Left Bank Bordeaux, but here the effects are heightened by both the Ciron River and Budos stream, plus a host of smaller underground water sources that provide a natural humidity to the soils and encourage both morning mists and afternoon rains. This makes Sauternes the perfect laboratory for the growth of botrytis rot.

Plant a red grape here and you'd be asking for trouble, but the protection offered by the immense Landes forest and the regular sunshine of south west France combines to do something magical to the sauvignon blanc, and more especially the sémillon grape. This is particularly true of the complex clay and sandy soils of Yquem, on a bedrock of limestone where the roots reach down close to 10 metres, encouraged by a series of drains first installed in 1884. The steeply sloped vineyards reach up to 80 meters above sea level at their highest point, the culminating point of the appellation, and head down to 40 metres above sea level at its lowest. It's the north-facing slopes of Block 43 at Yquem that are the most emblematic of the estate, where the drying effects of the winds are maximised and the soils are the strongest, most compacted clay that gives body, power and structure to the wine.

'Truly the soils themselves tell us what to grow,' says cellar master Sandrine Garbay. 'They ensure that at some point in the season, usually in early September as the grapes approach full ripeness, the grey rot is blocked by the drying impact of sun, heat and wind. A strong osmotic pressure stops this potentially devastating grey rot in its tracks, and it becomes instead a noble rot, brown not grey, that works its magic on the grapes.'

Magic is an over-used word, but the truth is that we have no idea how noble rot truly develops, nor exactly what mechanisms it unlocks. Its effect means the yields from the grapes are tiny – a fraction of that for red wine – but the liquid is concentrated, silky, aromatically explosive, and capable of ageing almost indefinitely. And it doesn't stop there.

'If the grapes aren't right in the field,' says Garbay, 'it doesn't matter what we do in the cellar. With red wines in challenging vintages you can select only the best grapes, or you can bleed off some juice during winemaking to concentrate what remains. There are plenty of tricks available in the cellar, but not here. There is a reason that we don't make Yquem in difficult years, why yields are so tiny even in the best vintages, and why the seductive complexity of the result is so unequalled in the pleasure that it brings.'

And perhaps that's the point. Masochists make this wine, hedonists drink it. Yquem shows us that we should never give up. Just because we are not good at one thing doesn't mean we won't be world-beating at something else. The possibility of redemption is inbuilt in every sip.

Size and production 279 acres, makes an average of 9,000 cases per year across Yquem and Y d'Yquem dry white. No second wine.
Owner Bernard Arnault's LVMH (investor since 1996, becoming the main shareholder in 1999).

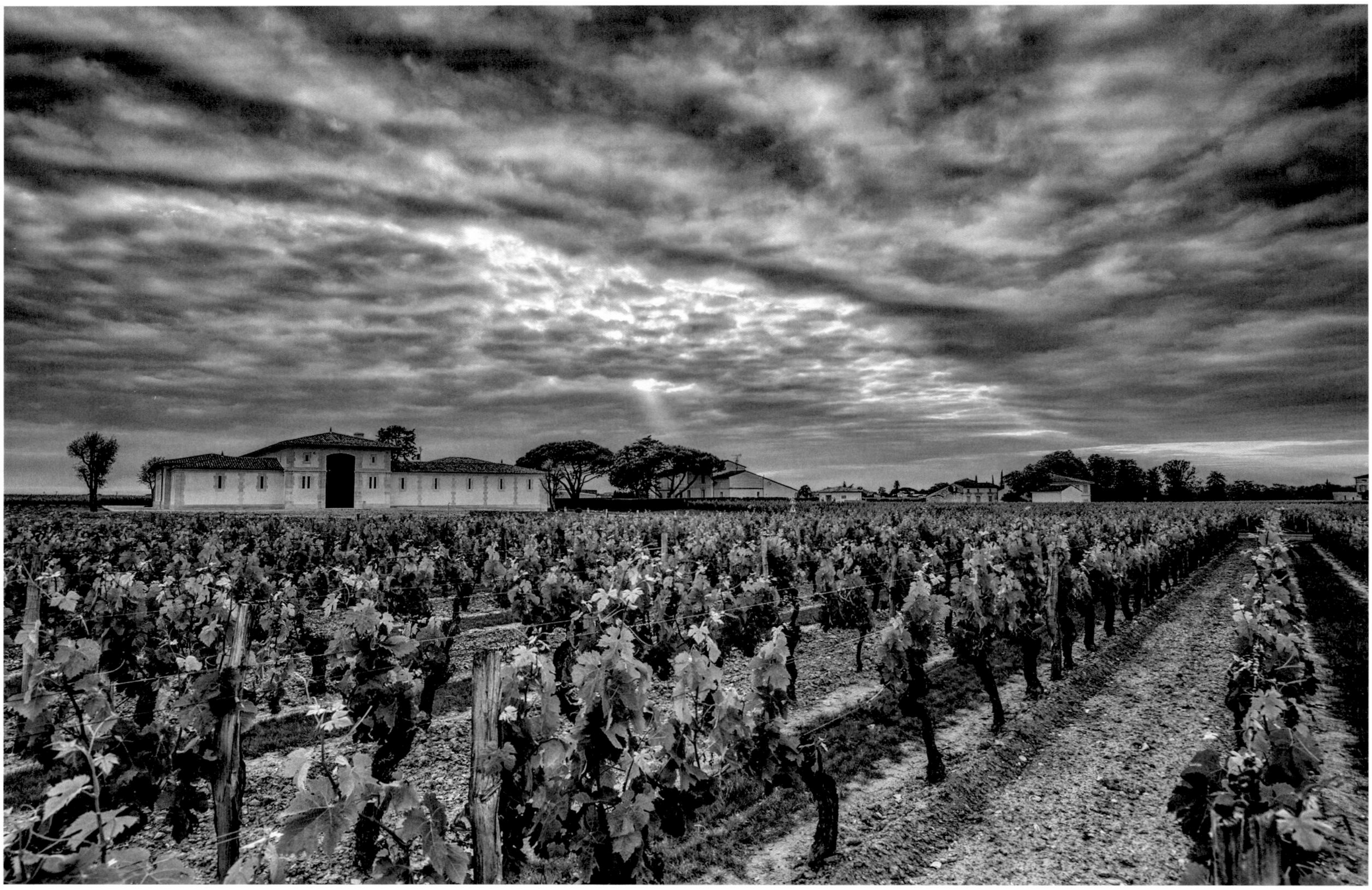

PETRUS AOC POMEROL

Pomerol is both the most egalitarian of appellations, because there are no classifications or rankings, and the most ruthlessly selective, because one name stands high above all others. The knock-out punch of two syllables: Petrus.

Petrus is a wine that displays the lightest of touches in transforming merlot, which can be such a powerful grape, into the deftest and most perfect of wine – fleshy, exotic and opulent, yet fragrant, silky and pure. This is where rich, spiced chocolate meets the delicacy of a redcurrant soufflé. The ultimate example of how great wines walk the tightrope between force and finesse. And how they become one of the most expensive liquids in the world by doing so.

This is not an easy thing to achieve with the rich power of merlot on the intense clay soils of Pomerol. We have crossed two rivers to get to this corner of Right Bank Bordeaux – first the Garonne, and then the Dordogne. We are now further from the oceanic influence of the Atlantic and the result is hotter, dryer summers and plump, luscious fruit.

'Our work is to resist temptation,' says winemaker Olivier Berrouet. 'Nature gives us so much at this spot, and our job is to simply express it without adding any adornments of our own. Wine comes from the heart of the grape, not the whole of it. Once we understand this, we understand everything.'

Petrus understands plenty about letting things speak for themselves. Of all the members of the Club of Nine, this is the estate that has found its global acclaim most recently. Unhurried, unforced, it was not wealthy aristocrats and political allegiances that brought this wine to prominence. It was simply the irrepressible force of an exceptional piece of land brought together, as ever, with somebody who believed in it unswervingly. Although it has been bottling under the name Petrus since the 18th century, its fame grew only in the late 1940s, when the Moueix family took over its distribution on behalf of then owner Madame Edmond Loubat. By the time they became sole owners, it was on an unstoppable trajectory. It became the holy grail for wine lovers: served at the wedding of Princess Elizabeth Windsor to Duke Phillip Mountbatten and a favourite in the Kennedy household in Washington DC.

The DNA of Petrus lies in its soils, and specifically its outcrop of 40 million year-old blue clay that is quite unlike the rest of Pomerol. Yes, you find clay everywhere here, but most of the neighbours have layers of gravel over the top. Here, for just over 19 of Petrus' 28 acres, the clay is pure, and of its own peculiar nature.

The Romans first named this place Petrus, meaning rock or stone, as a nod to the consistency of the earth in the heat of the sun. The solidity of the clay offers one reason why the vine roots only head down between one and two metres – far less than at some other properties and proof once again that there are no absolutes in greatness.

But this is, you've guessed it, no ordinary clay. Shot through with slivers of blue, by turns azure, cobalt and silvery grey, the clay here is dense and rich in iron. It expands rapidly in the rain, holding on to the water that gives it wonderfully protective qualities in the heat of summer. Yet it remains sticky enough to keep that water within its structure, maintaining the integrity of the soil and avoiding water-logging. No wet feet for the vines on this spot, and no need for the blending of grape varieties. Although there are traces of cabernet franc in the vineyard, used in the occasional vintage, Petrus is invariably almost 100% merlot.

'The crus of Bordeaux have an identity that comes out through the complexity of their soils,' says Berrouet, 'which is why blending grapes is such a skill in this region. Petrus is a little different because it is centred around the uniformity of the soil. Here are the personalities of one plot of land and one grape talking to each other, just as with pinot noir and the soils of Burgundy. We don't always know why they react to each other as they do, but it wasn't until merlot was the dominant grape here at the end of the 1800s that the true potential of this soil began to reveal itself.

'The interaction between plant and the organic and mineral elements in the soils is clearly extremely complex, but every sip of the final wine tells us that this blue clay nourishes the wine in its structure and aromatic potential, and delivers something extraordinary. Merlot is not always the easiest grape to work with. Its potential can be compromised by too much heat. It is sensitive to oxygen and to oak, malleable to the gestures of man. And yet if we guide rather then seek to control it, and if we allow the soils to speak through it rather than try to impose our own story, it has a magic that is unstoppable.'

Size and production 28 acres, makes an average of 2,500 cases per year. No second wine.
Owners Jean-François and Jean Moueix (Second and Third generation since Jean-Pierre Moueix purchased the property in 1969).

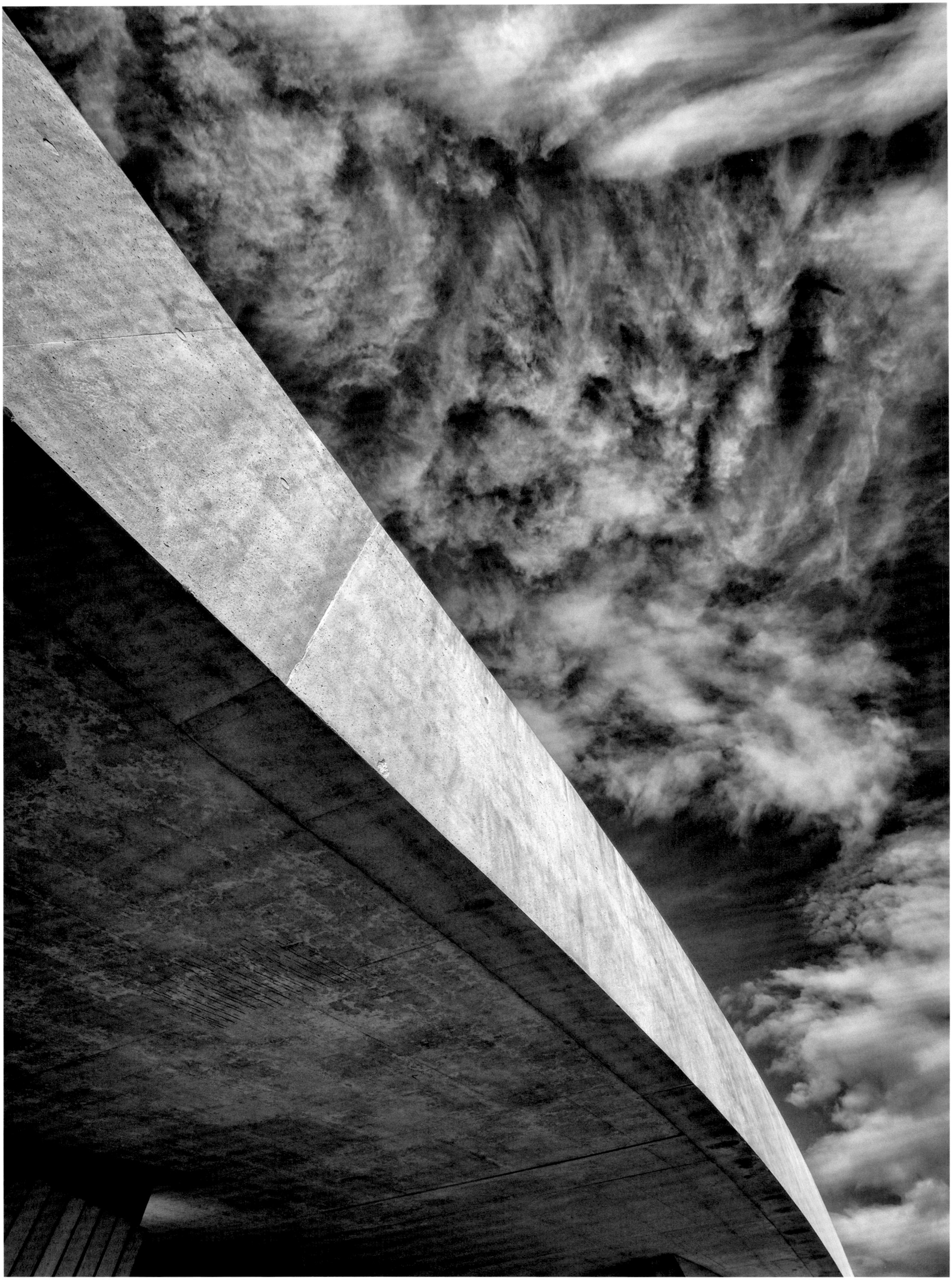

CHÂTEAU CHEVAL BLANC AOC SAINT EMILION PREMIER GRAND CRU CLASSÉ A

Cross the border from Pomerol into Saint Emilion and things are different once again. Where Petrus has one of the most homogeneous of all terroirs among these estates, Château Cheval Blanc has one of the most diverse. And where Petrus has no official ranking, Cheval Blanc has sat at the top of the Saint Emilion classification since its inception in the 1950s. Vines have been growing on this spot since at least the 1500s, and for more than 160 years Cheval Blanc has led the charge in Saint Emilion for a particular grape variety that is found in just 9% of Bordeaux vineyards today, but that is an integral part of the glory of this wine.

Here at Cheval there is none of the limestone terroir that Saint Emilion is most famed for. Instead the soils sit somewhere between those of Pomerol, with their rich clays, and those of Margaux, with an array of fine gravels that have flown along the Dordogne river from its source in the Massif Central mountain range. They explain why Cheval Blanc, with its equal parts of gravel and clay, has since the 1860s had almost half of the vineyard planted to merlot and the rest to the fragrant, elegant cabernet franc, finished off with just a fraction of cabernet sauvignon.

It is the dance between merlot and cabernet franc and their different expressions across the vineyard that makes Cheval Blanc, as winemaker Pierre-Olivier Clouet says, 'an orchestra not a soloist'.

'Our diversity is what gives such complexity,' he says. 'Our vineyard is split into 45 different plots according to soils, orientation, age of vines, grape variety or other factors. Some plots are small, with just a few dozen rows of vines, while others are significantly larger, but every single one has at some point been used in the production of our first wine over the past five years. Each one truly has something different to add to the overall picture of the wine, and each will respond slightly differently according to the weather conditions of the year. For us terroir is the composer and the vintage is the musician, interpreting what the composer is asking of it.'

Treating every single vine as a potential addition to the first wine – unlike in many Bordeaux estates, where certain vineyard blocks will never make it into the château's main bottling – means that the attention to detail in the vineyards throughout the year is unrivalled. Overseeing viticulture and technical direction is Kees van Leeuwen, a world-leading professor and terroir expert. Herbicide has never been used in the vineyard at Cheval Blanc, and the estate has its own vineyard nursery for practicing massal selection – the traditional method of propagating vines – using cuttings from old cabernet franc and merlot plants to ensure genetic diversity in the fields.

The beauty of Cheval Blanc is the balance that this mosaic of terroir gives; the feeling as you take a sip that you are paring back the layers one by one. Its success depends on the slow build of decision-making during the growing season, culminating in the year's most difficult decision: when to pick up the secateurs.

'The moment of deciding when to cut the grapes from the vine is the most crucial decision of the year,' says Clouet.

Harvesting is the moment of truth for all vineyards. It is also the moment of self-expression and self-determination. And here at Cheval it rests on three specific measurements. First: aromatics. Grapes, like all fruit, exhibit stages of ripeness that progress from green, or under ripe, through to ripe but still fresh, then on to overripe, shrivelled and, finally, rotten. The team at Cheval Blanc is interested in the stage of fresh fruit, when the integrity of skins is still in tact, the fruit still plump and mouth-watering.

Secondly: balance – the complex equation between acidity and sugar that marks out technological ripeness. Sugar is essential, clearly, as without it we have nothing to turn to alcohol during fermentation, but the grape needs to have retained enough acidity to keep the finished wine mouth-wateringly taut. And finally, the phenolic maturity of the tannins that ensures they're silky, fine, able to line the palate, glide through it without drying out.

From September each year, these measurements are assessed daily through analysis, observation and tasting during walks across each of the 45 plots. Picking will begin slowly, in stages, only when each grape is able to play its part in the creation of the first wine. Each plot is treated separately, according to its needs – a utopian dream that continues right through to the winery, where separate vats wait for each of the plots. Upon picking – by hand, naturally – any grapes that are underweight, under ripe or overripe will be discarded. Nothing is left to chance.

'The moment of harvest is when we fix the potential of the vintage,' says Clouet. 'All work in the cellars can have a negative impact after picking. Our job is to minimise the possibility of that, to not stand in the way of the work done by the soils, by the sunshine and by the grapes themselves.'

Size and production 101 acres, makes an average of 6,000 cases per year across Cheval Blanc and Petit Cheval.
Owners Albert Frère and Bernard Arnault (since 1998, with Arnault as owner through his company LVMH since 2009).

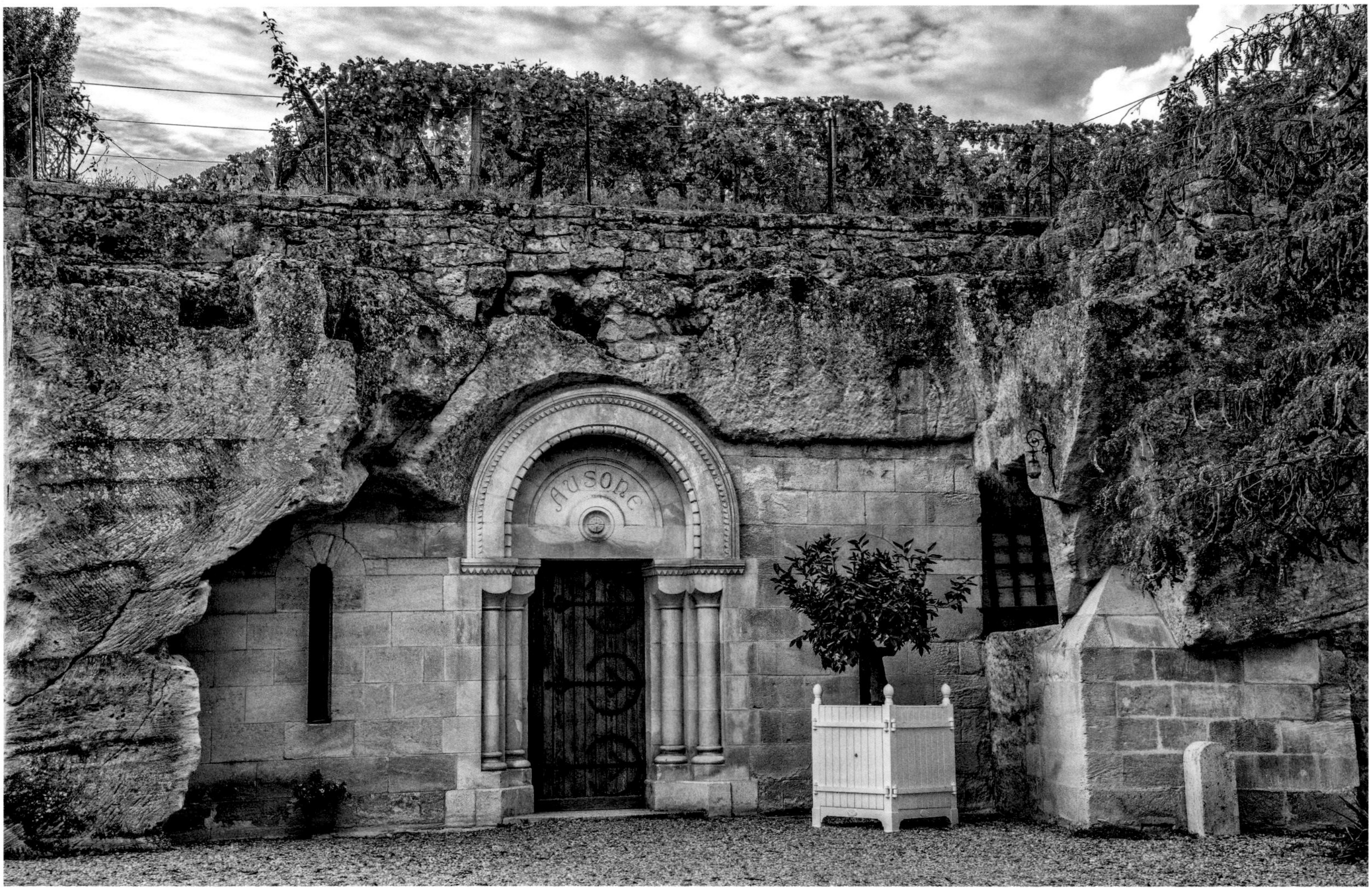
Ausone

CHÂTEAU AUSONE AOC SAINT EMILION PREMIER GRAND CRU CLASSÉ A

Limestone rules supreme in the medieval village of Saint Emilion. Its streets are lined with houses whose walls change colour from soft straw reflected in the morning sun to warm pink as the light deepens in the late afternoon.

Limestone quarries underpin the hill that the entire place is built on, and Europe's largest monolithic church lies under its market square. So much of its history and wealth is bound up in the extraction and use of the golden limestone – that takes its unusual colour from iron oxide – that it's no surprise that the beauty and finesse of its greatest wines are equally marked by it. And nowhere is this symbolised most clearly than at Château Ausone, an estate that sits way up at 75 metres above sea level on a limestone plateau shot through with a million fossilised oysters and seashells left behind by the waters that covered this spot around 30 million years ago.

'The magic of Ausone begins and ends with our terroir,' Pauline Vauthier, owner of Ausone, says. 'The Asteria limestone here is softer, more tender, than in many regions, making it the perfect sponge for drawing moisture away when too much rain falls and passing it back to the roots when conditions get too dry.'

Ausone, as with Cheval Blanc, has been a First Growth of Saint Emilion since the moment of the first ranking in the 1950s, and has a history that can be traced back at the very least to the 1200s when a château-fort stood on this spot.

Ausone is the smallest of the Club of Nine and the only one – Yquem comes a close second – with such steep slopes for its vines. Here the south-facing clay and limestone slopes fall away at a 20% gradient, making it extremely difficult to mechanise any part of the viticulture. Above them, on the flattened land in the former hamlet of La Madeleine, stands the winery, chapel and manor house, set back off a curve on a precipitously steep track above the entrance to the town.

Dry stone walls mark the edge of the vines – a romantic full-stop to the 17 acres planted at almost 5,000 vines per acre in parts of the vineyard, the highest density of the Firsts and particularly unusual for a Right Bank estate (although as vines are pulled up and replanted only very slowly here, Vauthier estimates that it will take 100 years before the entire vineyard is at this level). Here again cabernet franc dominates the blend, adding a rich exoticism to the flavour. Up to 65% of the vineyard at Ausone is given over to cabernet franc, with the oldest vines on limestone molassic slopes reaching 106 years old, showing just as with the cabernet sauvignon at Mouton Rothschild how long vines can live when they find their perfect terroir partner.

And sitting behind those slopes, accessed from just next to the chapel and heading down three levels underground, are the Ausone quarries. These quarries cover 8,000 square metres under the estate. They are among the oldest surviving examples of the 5,000 acres of quarries across the whole of Saint Emilion that provided wealth to the town for much of the 13th to 19th centuries. The earliest documents relating to quarries at Ausone date to 1568, and the lower levels alone gave around 20,000 square metres of stone for extraction, enough for 140 well-sized family houses. Pauline's father Alain Vauthier remembers running through these quarries as a child through the labyrinth of underground tunnels to the central square of Saint Emilion.

Today, the fragile lower tunnels are blocked off for safety, and only the first level is accessible. This is the smallest of the three, excavated at the end of the 16th century, with shell fossils specked through the rock walls and stone pillars holding up the four-metre high ceiling.

This cellar stands not only as a symbol of Saint Emilion's past but as a confident nod to its future. Because in these darkened rooms, with five centuries of history watching over them, between 100 and 200 barrels sleep, containing wine protected by an atmosphere with almost 95% relative humidity. This seriously deprives the angels of their share of the latest vintage of Ausone, but graciously leaves a larger slice for any of us lucky enough to have a glass ourselves.

Proof, as you find over and again with the Club of Nine, that these properties know how to harness the advantages offered by their environment, how to protect it for future generations, and how to learn from the lessons of history to better arm themselves for the challenges of tomorrow.

Size and production 17 acres, makes an average of 2,000 cases per year across Ausone and Chapelle d'Ausone.
Owner Alain Vaultier (Fourth generation since Edouard Dubois purchased the estate in 1892, full owner since 1997).

To the club of nine who welcomed
me like a member and to my favourite
winemaker my son Jesse Katz

First published in an edition of 2000 in 2016
by Katz eyes publication
andykatzphotography.com

For more information about this book
please visit the Andy Katz website.

Images © Andy Katz
Words © Jane Anson
Designed by SMITH
Allon Kaye, Claudia Paladini, Justine Schuster

Printed in Italy by EBS
ISBN 978-0-9649805-1-8

All Rights reserved. No part of this publication
may be reproduced, stored in a retrieval device
or transmitted in any other form or by any other
means, electrical, mechanical or otherwise,
without first seeking the permission of the
copyright owners and the publishers.